LAW, CRIME AND LAW ENFORCEMENT

FEDERAL PRISON INMATES

REHABILITATION AND EMPLOYMENT

LAW, CRIME AND LAW ENFORCEMENT

Additional books in this series can be found on Nova's website
under the Series tab.

Additional E-books in this series can be found on Nova's website
under the E-books tab.

LAW, CRIME AND LAW ENFORCEMENT

FEDERAL PRISON INMATES

REHABILITATION AND EMPLOYMENT

JENNIFER PAMETTO
AND
ERWIN JENKINS
EDITORS

Nova Science Publishers, Inc.
New York

Library of Congress Cataloging-in-Publication Data

Federal prison inmates : rehabilitation and employment / editors, Jennifer Pametto and Erwin Jenkins.
   p. cm.
Includes index.
ISBN 978-1-61470-120-0 (softcover)
1. Criminals--Rehabilitation--United States. 2. Prisoners--Employment--United States. 3. Prison industries--United States. 4. United States. Bureau of Prisons. I. Pametto, Jennifer. II. Jenkins, Erwin.
   HV9304.F423 2011
   365'.6610973--dc23
                              2011019870

Published by Nova Science Publishers, Inc. † New York

CONTENTS

Preface   vii

Chapter 1   About the Federal Bureau of Prisons   1
U.S. Department of Justice

Chapter 2   Federal Prison Inmates: Rehabilitative Needs and
Program Participation   15
Nathan James

Chapter 3   Federal Prison Industries   47
Nathan James

Chapter 4   Factories with Fences: 75 Years of Changing Lives   61
Jennifer Pametto and Erwin Jenkins

Chapter Sources   101

Index   103

PREFACE

The stated mission of the Bureau of Prisons (BOP) is "to protect society by confining offenders in the controlled environments of prisons and community-based facilities that are safe, humane, cost-efficient, and appropriately secure, and that provide work and other self-improvement opportunities to assist offenders in becoming law-abiding citizens." In support of this mission, BOP offers a variety of rehabilitative programs, including work opportunities through the Federal Prison Industries (FPI), occupational education programs, literacy/GED courses, and a variety of drug abuse treatment programs. This book examines the amount of resources available to BOP to carry out its mission to provide rehabilitative programming to federal inmates and the structure of incentives and effectiveness of inmates to participate in rehabilitative programming.

Chapter 1- The Federal Bureau of Prisons was established in 1930 to provide more progressive and humane care for Federal inmates, to professionalize the prison service, and to ensure consistent and centralized administration of the 11 Federal prisons in operation at that time. Today, the Bureau includes 116 institutions, 6 regional offices, a Central Office (headquarters), and community corrections offices that oversee residential reentry centers and home confinement programs. The regional offices and the Central Office provide administrative oversight and support to the institutions and community corrections offices.

Chapter 2- The stated mission of the Bureau of Prisons (BOP) is "to protect society by confining offenders in the controlled environments of prisons and community-based facilities that are safe, humane, cost-efficient, and appropriately secure, and that provide work and other self-improvement opportunities to assist offenders in becoming law-abiding citizens." In support of this mission, BOP offers a variety of rehabilitative programs, including work opportunities through the Federal Prison Industries (FPI), occupational education programs, literacy/GED courses, and a variety of drug abuse treatment programs.

Chapter 3- UNICOR, the trade name for Federal Prison Industries, Inc. (FPI), is a government-owned corporation that employs offenders incarcerated in correctional facilities under the Federal Bureau of Prisons (BOP). UNICOR manufactures products and provides services that are sold to executive agencies in the federal government. FPI was created to serve as a means for managing, training, and rehabilitating inmates in the federal prison system through employment in one of its industries.

In: Federal Prison Inmates
Editors: J. Pametto and E. Jenkins

ISBN: 978-1-61470-120-0
© 2011 Nova Science Publishers, Inc.

Chapter 1

ABOUT THE FEDERAL BUREAU OF PRISONS

U.S. Department of Justice

The Federal Bureau of Prisons was established in 1930 to provide more progressive and humane care for Federal inmates, to professionalize the prison service, and to ensure consistent and centralized administration of the 11 Federal prisons in operation at that time. Today, the Bureau includes 116 institutions, 6 regional offices, a Central Office (headquarters), and community corrections offices that oversee residential reentry centers and home confinement programs. The regional offices and the Central Office provide administrative oversight and support to the institutions and community corrections offices.

The Bureau is responsible for the custody and care of more than 209,500 Federal offenders. Approximately 82 percent of these inmates are confined in Bureau-operated correctional institutions or detention centers. The remainder is confined in secure privately managed or community-based facilities and local jails.

The Bureau protects public safety by ensuring Federal offenders serve their sentences of imprisonment in institutions that are safe, humane, cost-efficient, and appropriately secure. The Bureau helps reduce future criminal activity by encouraging inmates to participate in a range of programs that have been proven to help them adopt a crime-free lifestyle upon their return to the community.

Federal Correctional Institution.

The Bureau's most important resource is its staff. The more than 38,500 employees of the Bureau of Prisons ensure the security of Federal prisons, provide inmates with needed programs and services, and model mainstream values. The Bureau's employees help the agency meet its obligation to protect public safety and provide security and safety to the staff and inmates in its facilities.

GROWTH OF THE FEDERAL INMATE POPULATION

Most of the challenges affecting the Bureau today relate to the agency's growth. At the end of 1930 (the year the Bureau was created), the agency operated 14 institutions for just over 13,000 inmates. In 1940, the Bureau had grown to 24 institutions with 24,360 inmates. Except for a few fluctuations, the number of inmates did not change significantly between 1940 and 1980 (when the population was 24,252). However, during this same time period, the number of institutions almost doubled (from 24 to 44) as the Bureau gradually moved from operating large institutions confining inmates of many security levels to operating smaller facilities that each confined inmates with similar security needs.

As a result of Federal law enforcement efforts and new legislation that dramatically altered sentencing in the Federal criminal justice system, the 1 980s brought a significant increase in the number of Federal inmates. In fact, most of the Bureau's growth from the mid-1980s to the late 1990s was the result of the Sentencing Reform Act of 1984 (which established determinate sentencing, abolished parole, and reduced good time) and mandatory minimum sentences enacted in 1986, 1988, and 1990. From 1980 to 1989, the inmate population more than doubled, from just over 24,000 to almost 58,000. During the 1990s, the population more than doubled again, reaching approximately 136,000 at the end of 1999 as efforts to combat illegal drugs, weapons, and immigration contributed to significantly increased numbers of inmates.

The Bureau projects continued population growth over the next several years. The agency is preparing for this growth through construction of new institutions, expansions at some existing facilities, and increased contracting for the housing of low security criminal aliens.

INSTITUTION SECURITY

The Bureau ensures institution security through a combination of direct staff supervision, physical features, security technologies, and classification of inmates based on risk factors. The Bureau operates institutions at four security levels (minimum, low, medium, and high) to meet the various security needs of its diverse inmate population and has one maximum-security prison for the less than one percent of the inmates who require that level of security. It also has administrative facilities, such as pretrial detention centers and medical referral centers, that have specialized missions and confine offenders of all security levels. The characteristics that help define the security level of an institution are perimeter security measures (such as fences, patrol officers, and towers), the level of staffing, the internal controls for inmate movement and accountability, and the type of inmate living quarters (for example, cells or open dormitories). The Bureau's graduated security and medical classification schemes allow staff to assign an inmate to an institution in accordance with the inmate's individual needs. Thus, inmates who are able to function with relatively less supervision, without disrupting institution operations or threatening the safety of staff, other inmates, or the public, can be housed in lower security level institutions.

Regardless of the specific discipline in which a staff member works, all employees are "correctional workers first." This means everyone is responsible for the security and good order of the institution. All staff are expected to be vigilant and attentive to inmate accountability and security issues, to respond to emergencies, and to maintain a proficiency in custodial and security matters, as well as in their particular job specialty. This approach allows the Bureau to operate in the most cost-effective manner with fewer correctional officers and still maintain direct supervision of inmates; it also maximizes emergency preparedness.

Architecture and technological innovations help the Bureau maintain the safety and security of its institutions; and the Bureau routinely evaluates emerging technologies to determine which might further improve the physical security of its institutions. To facilitate direct supervision of inmates, the Bureau has eliminated structural barriers (such as bars and grilles) between staff and inmates where possible. In addition, many staff offices are located near areas where programs and services are delivered. Staff circulate freely and constantly through all areas of the institution, continually interacting with inmates. This promotes a more normalized environment within the institution, with staff serving as law-abiding role models, and places staff in a better position to observe and respond to inmate behavior. Many institutions also rely on surveillance through CCTV cameras to augment direct staff supervision of inmates.

INMATE MANAGEMENT

Staff are the key component to effective inmate management. Constructive and frequent interaction and communication between staff and inmates are critical to maintaining accountability, ensuring security, and managing inmate behavior. Bureau staff are expected to talk with and be available to inmates and to be receptive to inmate concerns.

Correctional workers performing routine duties.

Unit management is one hallmark of the Bureau's inmate management philosophy. Unit management gives inmates direct daily contact with the staff who make most of the decisions about their daily lives. These staff (the unit manager, case manager, and correctional counselor) have offices in inmate living units, thereby facilitating inmate access to staff and vice versa. This also facilitates identification of significant inmate concerns and potential problems.

Unit staff are directly responsible for involving inmates, who housed in their units, in programs that are designed to meet their needs. Unit staff receive input from other institution employees (such as work supervisors, teachers, and psychologists) who work with the inmate, and meet with the inmate on a regular basis to develop, review, and discuss their work assignment, appropriate program opportunities, and progress, as well as any other needs or concerns. These regularly-scheduled meetings do not preclude inmates from approaching a member of the unit team or any other appropriate staff member at any time to discuss their particular issues.

Bureau staff are the inmates' primary role models during their incarceration, and the Bureau emphasizes employee ethics, responsibility, and standards of conduct. The Bureau expects its employees to conduct themselves in a manner that creates and maintains respect for the agency, the Department of Justice, the Federal Government, and the law. Bureau employees are expected to avoid situations that create conflicts of interest with their employment and to uphold and comply with the ethical rules and standards that govern their specific professions, as well as the laws, regulations, and procedures that ensure institution security and protect the safety of inmates and the general public.

Another significant way the Bureau maintains security and the safety of staff and inmates is by keeping inmates constructively occupied. Meeting the challenges posed by an increasing and changing inmate population involves more than just providing bedspace, meals, and health care. Correctional programs and activities not only reduce inmate idleness and the stresses associated with living in a prison, but also play a major role in preparing inmates for their eventual return to the community.

INMATE PROGRAMS

The Bureau also has a responsibility to provide inmates with opportunities to participate in programs that can provide them with the skills they need to lead crime-free lives after release. The Bureau's philosophy is that release preparation begins the first day of imprisonment. Accordingly, the Bureau provides many self-improvement programs, including work in prison industries and other institution jobs, vocational training, education, substance abuse treatment, parenting, anger management, counseling, religious observance opportunities, and other programs that teach essential life skills. The Bureau also provides other structured activities designed to teach inmates productive ways to use their time.

Through its Inmate Skills Development initiative, the Bureau has identified those skills (e.g., daily living, interpersonal, and cognitive skills) that appear to be essential to successful community reintegration. Identifying an inmate's strengths and weaknesses allows Bureau staff to guide the inmate to selectively work on improving deficit areas. By targeting inmates' specific need areas, the Bureau strives to maximize programming effectiveness for each inmate, thereby improving the likelihood of success upon release.

Prison work programs provide inmates an opportunity to acquire marketable occupational skills, as well as learn and practice sound work ethic and habits. All sentenced inmates in Federal correctional institutions are required to work (with the exception of those who for security, educational, or medical reasons are unable to do so). Most inmates are assigned to an institutional job such as a food service worker, orderly, plumber, painter, warehouse worker, or groundskeeper.

Federal Prison Industries (FPI) is one of the Bureau's most important correctional programs. It significantly reduces recidivism and contributes to institution security and safety by engaging inmates in constructive activities. The goal is to have 25 percent of the Bureau's eligible sentenced inmates work in FPI factories. They gain job skills through specific instruction in factory operations related to a variety of product lines and services. Inmates are compensated for their work and can receive raises based on their performance.

Inmates confined in Bureau facilities can also access a broad range of other programming opportunities. For example, Bureau institutions offer religious services and programs for the approximately 30 faith groups represented within the inmate population. Inmates are granted permission to wear or retain various religious items, and accommodations are made to facilitate observances of holy days. Bureau facilities offer religious diets designed to meet the dietary requirements of various faith groups, such as the Jewish and Islamic faiths. Most institutions have sweat lodges to accommodate the religious requirements of those whose religious preference is Native American. Religious programs are led or supervised by staff chaplains, contract spiritual leaders, and community volunteers. Chaplains oversee inmate worship services and self-improvement programs, such as those involving the study of sacred writings and religious workshops. Bureau chaplains also provide pastoral care, spiritual guidance, and counseling to inmates. Inmates may request visits and spiritual counseling from community representatives. Additionally, the Bureau offers inmates the opportunity to participate in its Life Connections Program, a residential re-entry program implemented by the Religious Services Branch in partnership with various faith communities nationwide.

Inmates working in Federal Prison Industries factory.

Inmates are considered responsible for their own behavior, including that which led to their incarceration, and therefore, they are strongly encouraged to participate in self-improvement programs that will provide them with the skills they need to conduct themselves as productive, law-abiding citizens upon release. Inmates show responsibility through their behavior and conduct in prison, through active and constructive involvement in programs, and by living up to their financial commitments and responsibilities. The Bureau encourages inmates to help meet their family and financial obligations with their earnings from work or other financial assets. The Inmate Financial Responsibility Program requires inmates to make payments from their earnings to satisfy court-ordered fines, victim restitution, child support, and other monetary judgments. The majority of the court-ordered fine and restitution money goes to crime victims or victim support organizations.

Inmate programs include spiritual counseling.

Inmates are considered responsible for their own behavior, including that which led to their incarceration, and therefore, they are strongly encouraged to participate in self-improvement programs that will provide them with the skills they need to conduct themselves as productive, law-abiding citizens upon release. Inmates show responsibility through their behavior and conduct in prison, through active and constructive involvement in programs, and by living up to their financial commitments and responsibilities. The Bureau encourages inmates to help meet their family and financial obligations with their earnings from work or other financial assets. The Inmate Financial Responsibility Program requires inmates to make payments from their earnings to satisfy court-ordered fines, victim restitution, child support, and other monetary judgments. The majority of the court-ordered fine and restitution money goes to crime victims or victim support organizations.

The Bureau strives to create an environment for inmates that is conducive to change. In addition, Bureau facilities are well-maintained, clean, and orderly in order to provide inmates and staff a healthy, normalized living and working environment.

IMPROVING INMATES' LIVES AND REDUCING RECIDIVISM

Research shows that industrial work programs, vocational training, education, and drug treatment in prison play a major role in improving public safety. These programs reduce recidivism and misconduct in prison. Drug treatment programs also decrease offenders' relapse to drug use after release. Many correctional systems, including the Bureau, have documented the success of these programs.

The Post-Release Employment Project

The Post-Release Employment Project is a long-term study designed to evaluate the impact of FPI prison industrial work experience (alone and in conjunction with vocational and apprenticeship training) on former Federal inmates' post-release adjustment. A significant early finding of the research was that FPI program participants showed better institutional adjustment -- they were less likely to be involved in misconduct and, when involved, misconduct was less severe. Early data analysis also focused on the ex-inmates' first year in the community. (The first year after release from prison is critical to successful reintegration and to remaining crime free.) The major findings at the one-year follow-up point were that FPI program participants: (1) were significantly less likely to recidivate (i.e., be rearrested or have their post-confinement community supervision revoked) than comparison group members, (2) were more likely to be employed during their first year after release, and (3) earned slightly higher wages, on average, during the first year after release.

Ongoing research has found that, as many as 8 to 12 years after their release, inmates who worked in prison industries were 24 percent less likely to recidivate than inmates who did not participate. The results further indicated that work program participants were 14 percent more likely to be employed following release from prison than those who did not participate. In addition, minority groups that are at greatest risk for recidivism benefitted more from industrial work participation and vocational training than their non-minority counterparts. Inmates who participated in either vocational or apprenticeship training were 33 percent less likely to recidivate than inmates who did not participate.

Education

Participation in education programs also has a positive effect on post-release success. The findings showed a significant decline in recidivism rates among inmates who completed one or more educational courses during any six-month period of their imprisonment.

Residential Substance Abuse Treatment

Residential drug abuse treatment programs (RDAPs) are offered at more than 60 Bureau institutions, providing treatment to more than 17,000 inmates each year. Inmates who participate in these residential programs are housed together in a separate unit of the prison reserved for drug treatment. RDAPs provide intensive half-day programming, 5 days a week, for 9 months. The remainder of each day is spent in education, work skills training, and other inmate programs.

According to the results of a rigorous study of the effect of residential drug treatment, male and female inmates who completed RDAP and were released to the community for at least 3 years were significantly less likely to recidivate and significantly less likely to relapse to drug use, as compared to similar non-participating inmates. The study also found improved employment among women after release. In addition, an evaluation of inmate behavior found that institution misconduct among male inmates who completed RDAP was reduced by 25 percent when compared to misconduct among similar non-participating male inmates; and institution misconduct among female inmates who completed residential treatment was reduced by 70 percent. These results demonstrate that residential drug abuse treatment in corrections-based settings makes a significant difference in the lives of inmates following their release from custody and yields a significant benefit to institution safety and security.

Specific Pro-Social Values Programs

Encouraged by RDAP's positive results, the Bureau implemented a number of other residential programs for special populations (including younger offenders, high- security inmates, and intractable, quick-tempered inmates) that are responsible for much of the misconduct that occurs in Federal prisons. The cognitive restructuring approach used in the drug treatment programs served as the foundation for programs designed to change the criminal thinking and behavior patterns of inmates. These programs focus on inmates' emotional and behavioral responses to difficult situations and emphasize life skills and the development of pro-social values, respect for self and others, responsibility for personal actions, and tolerance. Each program was developed with an evaluation component to ensure the program meets the goals of promoting positive behavior. While it is too early to assess the programs' effects in terms of reducing recidivism, the Bureau has found that these cognitive restructuring programs significantly reduce inmates' involvement in institution misconduct.

Preparing Inmates for Release

Inmate program involvement is ultimately geared toward helping inmates prepare for their eventual release. The Bureau complements its array of programs with a specific Release Preparation Program, with inmate participation occuring near the end of his/her sentence. This program includes classes on resume writing, job search strategies, and job retention. It also includes presentations by representatives from community-based organizations that help ex-inmates find employment and training opportunities after release from prison. The Bureau places most inmates in residential reentry centers (also known as halfway houses) prior to their release from custody in order to help them adjust to life in the community and find suitable post-release employment.

The Bureau's Inmate Transition Branch provides additional post-release employment assistance to inmates. It helps inmates prepare release portfolios that include a resume, education and training certificates and transcripts, diplomas, and other significant documents needed for a successful job interview. Many institutions hold mock job fairs to provide inmates an opportunity to practice and improve job interview techniques and to expose community recruiters to the skills available among inmates. Qualified inmates may apply for jobs with companies that have job openings.

COMMUNITY-BASED CONFINEMENT
AND COMMUNITY ACTIVITIES

Residential reentry centers (RRCs) are used by the Bureau to place inmates in the community just prior to their release. These centers provide a structured, supervised environment and support in job placement, counseling, and other services. They make it possible for inmates to gradually rebuild their ties to the community and allow correctional staff to supervise offenders' activities during this important readjustment phase. Inmates in RRCs are required to work and to pay a subsistence charge of 25 percent of their income to defray the cost of confinement. Some Federal inmates are placed in home confinement for a brief period at the end of their prison terms. They serve this portion of their sentences at home under strict schedules, curfew requirements, telephonic monitoring, and sometimes electronic monitoring.

Through public works projects, some minimum security inmates from Federal Prison Camps perform labor-intensive work off institutional grounds for other Federal entities, such as the National Park Service, the U.S. Forest Service, and the U.S. armed services. These inmates work at their job site during the day and return to the institution at the end of the work day.

Some carefully-selected Federal inmates speak to youth groups at schools, universities, juvenile offender programs, and drug treatment programs to give juveniles and young adults a first-hand understanding of the consequences of drug use and crime. Other inmates volunteer to help the communities near their institution, providing services that otherwise would not likely be performed, such as repairing or rebuilding dilapidated buildings and cleaning up or beautifying streets, roadsides, parks, schools, ball fields, and other public grounds.

Under limited circumstances, inmates who meet strict requirements are allowed temporary releases from the institution through staff-escorted trips and furloughs. The Bureau permits approved inmates to go on staff-escorted trips into the community to visit a critically-ill member of their immediate family; attend the funeral of an immediate family member; receive medical treatment; or participate in other activities, such as a religious or work-related functions.

A furlough is a temporary authorization for an appropriate inmate to be in the community without a staff escort. Inmates near the end of their sentences who require minimal security may be granted permission to go on trips into the community without escort to be present during a crisis in the immediate family, to participate in certain activities that will facilitate release transition, and to re-establish family and community ties. Furloughs are not very common, and inmates are carefully screened for risk to the community before they are released on a furlough.

Research has shown that inmates who maintain ties with their families have reduced recidivism rates. Accordingly, the Bureau helps inmates maintain their family and community ties through visiting, mail, and telephone privileges. The Bureau allows social visits with approved family and friends. The Bureau does not permit conjugal visits.

COMMUNITY INVOLVEMENT WITH INMATES AND THE BUREAU

The Bureau welcomes community involvement in its institutions and offices. Volunteers help inmates adapt successfully to imprisonment and prepare for their eventual adjustment into the community after release. Volunteers provide a variety of services, such as spiritual counseling, assistance with family and marriage issues, substance abuse counseling, education and vocational training, and health education.

Most institutions have Community Relations Boards that facilitate information flow between the facility and the local community, advancing public awareness and an understanding of any issues of concern at the prison. All Federal prisons have arrangements with state and local law enforcement agencies and other emergency services in the rare event of an escape or other security concern. Bureau institutions are involved in a variety of joint training activities with state, local, and other Federal law enforcement agencies; they often allow these agencies to use training areas in their institutions.

THE IMAGE OF CORRECTIONS

Unfortunately, the general public often forms its impressions of prisons and correctional systems from mass media sources like movies or the news. Movies about prisons are frequently gross misrepresentations of reality. For example, *White Heat, Bird Man of Alcatraz, Cool Hand Luke,* and *The Shawshank Redemption* are fictional depictions of prison life. These movies, and many others, exaggerate life within a prison and tend to cast prison operations and administrators in a negative light.

Those who draw their impressions of prisons from movies alone may think of them as brutal environments with corrupt or incompetent staff who inflict needless cruelty on inmates. Others may think of prisons as unduly luxurious places that provide needless "amenities" at the expense of the taxpaying public. Still others come to conclusions based on documentaries of famous prisons, such as Alcatraz, or on news reports that tend to highlight an unfortunate, isolated event and make it appear as if it is representative of an entire correctional system.

The Bureau of Prisons prides itself on being an outstanding public service organization, that works diligently to achieve its goals of ensuring public safety and providing appropriate, efficient, safe, and humane correctional services and programs.

For further information, contact the Federal Bureau of Prisons at (202) 307-3198 or visit the Bureau's website at www.bop.gov.

In: Federal Prison Inmates
Editors: J. Pametto and E. Jenkins

ISBN: 978-1-61470-120-0
© 2011 Nova Science Publishers, Inc.

Chapter 2

FEDERAL PRISON INMATES: REHABILITATIVE NEEDS AND PROGRAM PARTICIPATION

Nathan James

SUMMARY

The stated mission of the Bureau of Prisons (BOP) is "to protect society by confining offenders in the controlled environments of prisons and community-based facilities that are safe, humane, cost-efficient, and appropriately secure, and that provide work and other self-improvement opportunities to assist offenders in becoming law-abiding citizens." In support of this mission, BOP offers a variety of rehabilitative programs, including work opportunities through the Federal Prison Industries (FPI), occupational education programs, literacy/GED courses, and a variety of drug abuse treatment programs.

CRS used data from the 1997 and 2004 *Survey of Inmates in State and Federal Correctional Facilities* to analyze (1) whether there has been an increase in the proportion of federal inmates in need of rehabilitative programming, (2) if inmates with a need for rehabilitative programming were more likely than other inmates to participate in a program to address their need, and (3) whether there was an increase between 1997 and 2004 in the probability that inmates with a reported need participated in rehabilitative programming.

Some of the key findings from the CRS analysis include the following: (1) data from the 1997 and 2004 surveys show that it was likely that there was increased need for drug abuse treatment programs, but the need for literacy/GED and occupational education programs along with FPI work assignments remained flat; (2) with the exception of inmates who were unemployed before being arrested, inmates who had a rehabilitative need were significantly more likely than other inmates to participate in a rehabilitative program to address their need; (3) there was not a significant difference in the likelihood that inmates in 1997 and 2004 with rehabilitative needs participated in programming; and (4) the probability that a typical inmate with a rehabilitative need participated in a program to address that need was, in most cases, less than 1 in 2, and the probability that the highest-participating inmates participated in rehabilitative programs was 3 in 5 or lower.

Potential issues relevant to this analysis include the amount of resources available to BOP to carry out its mission to provide rehabilitative programming to federal inmates and the structure of incentives for inmates to participate in rehabilitative programs.

INTRODUCTION

The stated mission of the Bureau of Prisons (BOP) is "to protect society by confining offenders in the controlled environments of prisons and community-based facilities that are safe, humane, cost-efficient, and appropriately secure, and that *provide work and other self-improvement opportunities to assist offenders in becoming law-abiding citizens*" (emphasis added).[1] Rehabilitative programs not only prevent inmate idleness, they also form a part of an effective reentry strategy for inmates.[2]

CRS used data from the 1997 and 2004 *Survey of Inmates in State and Federal Correctional Facilities* to analyze (1) whether there has been an increase in the proportion of federal inmates in need of rehabilitative programming, (2) if inmates with a need for rehabilitative programming were more likely than other inmates to participate in a program to address their need, and (3) whether there was an increase between 1997 and 2004 in the probability that inmates with a reported need participated in rehabilitative programming.

Potential issues relevant to this analysis include the amount of resources available to BOP to carry out its mission to provide rehabilitative programming to federal inmates and the structure of incentives for inmates to participate in rehabilitative programs.

The report starts with a brief overview of BOP, followed by a description of BOP 's main rehabilitative programs. Next, there is a short review of the research on the effectiveness of rehabilitative programming. The report then turns to the analysis described above. The report concludes with a discussion of selected issues for Congress.

THE BUREAU OF PRISONS (BOP)

BOP is a component of the Department of Justice (DOJ), and it is responsible for the custody and care of all federal prisoners.[3] BOP was established in 1930 to house federal inmates, to professionalize the prison service, and to ensure consistent and centralized administration of the federal prison system.[4] At the end of 1930, BOP operated 14 facilities for just over 13,000 inmates.[5] By 1940, BOP opened 10 additional prisons while the federal prison population grew by approximately 11,000 inmates. According to BOP, the number of inmates did not change significantly between 1940 and 1980.[6] However, during this time period the number of prisons operated by BOP almost doubled as it moved from operating large prisons confining inmates of many security levels to operating smaller prisons that confined inmates with similar security needs.

BOP currently operates 116 correctional facilities, housing approximately 173,000 inmates.[7] BOP reports that approximately 80% of inmates under its jurisdiction are housed in BOP-operated facilities; the remainder are housed in contract facilities (i.e., privately managed secure or community-based facilities or local jails).[8] All BOP correctional facilities are classified according to one of five different security levels: minimum, low, medium, high, or administrative. A facility's security level is based on the facility's features, which include the presence of external patrols, towers, security barriers, or detection devices; the type of housing within the institution; internal security features; and the staff-to-inmate ratio.[9]

BOP also contracts with Residential Re-entry Centers (RRCs) (i.e., halfway houses) to provide assistance to inmates nearing release.[10] RRCs provide inmates with a structured and supervised environment along with employment counseling, job placement services, financial management assistance, and other programs and services.[11] RRCs facilitate inmates' efforts at reestablishing ties to the community while allowing correctional staff to supervise inmates' activities.[12] According to BOP, its goal is to place inmates in RRCs for the amount of time necessary to provide the greatest likelihood of successful reentry into the community.

BOP's REHABILITATIVE PROGRAMS

BOP provides a variety of rehabilitative programs for federal prison inmates, three of which are the focus of this report: work assignments through the Federal Prison Industries (FPI),[13] educational programs, and substance abuse treatment. Each program is discussed in more detail below.

Federal Prison Industries (FPI)[14]

It is BOP 's policy that all sentenced inmates are required to work if they are medically able. According to BOP, work programs assist with inmate management by reducing idleness and they teach inmates skills and the importance of a good work ethic. Inmates can work in either institutional work assignments or FPI factories.[15] For both institutional work assignments and FPI factory jobs, a high school diploma or a General Equivalency Diploma (GED) is required for all work assignments above entry level.

Inmates working in FPI jobs are paid between $0.23 and $1.15 per hour. All inmates or detainees may be considered for an FPI job unless the inmate is a pretrial inmate or is currently under an order of deportation, exclusion, or removal. Inmates working in FPI factories are also eligible, as earnings permit, to participate in training that relates directly to the inmate's job assignment. Inmates selected to participate in FPI-funded job training must have enough time left on their sentences to allow them to complete the training. FPI also provides scholarships to allow inmates to begin, or continue, postsecondary business and industry courses or vocational training. According to BOP, 11.0% of inmates had an FPI work assignment in FY2009.

Education Programs

BOP provides inmates with a variety of education programs, including the Literacy/GED program, the Occupational Education program, the English-as-a-Second Language program, and the Postsecondary Education program. This report focuses on the Literacy/GED and Occupational Education programs because they are the two programs inmates are the most likely to participate in.

Literacy/GED[16]

Under current law, BOP is required to both provide a functional literacy program for all mentally capable inmates who are not functionally literate and to offer literacy/GED programs for inmates who have not earned a high school diploma or its equivalent.[17] In addition, federal inmates are required to make satisfactory progress toward earning a high school diploma or a GED in order to earn their full allotment of good time credit.[18]

BOP's literacy program is designed to help inmates develop reading, math, and writing skills, and to prepare inmates for earning a GED credential. With few exceptions (e.g., pretrial inmates, inmates committed for the purpose of observation, inmates determined by the staff to be temporarily unable to participate in the literacy program due to circumstances beyond their control, and sentenced deportable aliens), all sentenced inmates without a high school diploma or a GED are required to enroll in the adult literacy program for a minimum of 240 hours or until a GED is earned, whichever comes first.

After completing the required 240 hours of instructional time in the literacy program, an inmate may elect to discontinue participation in the literacy program.[19] However, if an inmate chooses to opt out of the literacy program after completing 240 hours of instructional time, it can affect the inmate's ability to earn the full allotment of good time credit. Also, not continuing in the literacy program, or not earning a GED, can limit the type of work assignments an inmate can receive. According to BOP, 12.5% of federal inmates participated in a literacy/GED course in FY2009.

Occupational Education Program[20]

BOP provides an occupational education program at nearly all of its correctional facilities. To participate in an occupational education program, an inmate must have a high school diploma, have earned a GED, or be concurrently enrolled in a GED program.

Occupational education programs may include the following types of training:

- **Exploratory training:** Exploratory training is a study of occupations and industries for the purpose of providing the inmate with a general knowledge of an occupation and the work world. This type of training does not provide specific skill development.

- **Marketable training:** Marketable training provides inmates with the skills necessary to work in an entry-level position in a specific occupation or a related group of occupational fields. Marketable training can include "live work," meaning that the work results in a product or service for use by the correctional institution, FPI, another federal agency, or a community service project.
- **Apprentice training:** Apprentice training provides inmates with the opportunity to train for post-release employment in various trades. The Bureau of Apprenticeship Training (BAT) works with the institution's education staff to develop registered apprenticeship programs.

Inmates may be required to make a co-payment to enroll and participate in an occupational education program. Co-payments are limited to the cost of books for the courses. According to BOP, 6.5% of federal inmates participated in an occupational education course in FY2009.

Drug Abuse Treatment Programs[21]

Current law (18 U.S.C. § 3621) requires BOP to provide, subject to appropriations, residential substance abuse treatment[22] and appropriate aftercare[23] for all eligible prisoners.[24] Prisoners who are convicted of nonviolent crimes who successfully complete a residential substance abuse treatment program can have their sentence reduced by not more than one year.[25]

BOP's policy is to interview all new inmates to screen them for drug abuse problems. BOP also reviews each inmate's records for evidence of drug abuse. Based on the interview and record review, BOP staff makes a drug education/treatment referral. BOP offers four types of drug abuse treatment to federal inmates: (1) a drug abuse education course, (2) non-residential drug abuse treatment, (3) residential drug abuse treatment, and (4) community transition drug abuse treatment. Each program is discussed in more detail below.

Drug Abuse Education Course

A drug abuse education course is offered at all BOP institutions. Inmates are required to participate in a drug abuse education course when they have been sentenced or returned to custody because of a parole or supervised release violation after September 30, 1991, and it is determined that (1) there is evidence in the presentence investigation report that alcohol or other drug abuse contributed to the offense; (2) alcohol or other drug use was the reason for the violation of supervised release, parole, or conditions of RRC placement or home confinement; or (3) the inmate was recommended for drug abuse treatment programming by the sentencing judge.

The course informs inmates about the relationship between drug abuse and crime and the psychological, physical, and social impact of abusing drugs and alcohol. It is also designed to motivate inmates who need additional drug abuse treatment to participate in non-residential or residential drug abuse treatment. Inmates not required to participate in the drug abuse education course may volunteer to participate when space is available. According to BOP, 17.8% of inmates participated in a drug abuse education treatment program in FY2009.

Non-residential Drug Abuse Treatment

Like the drug abuse education course, non-residential drug abuse treatment is available at all BOP institutions. Participation in the institution's non-residential drug abuse treatment program is voluntary. According to BOP, non-residential drug abuse treatment is designed with the flexibility necessary to meet the treatment needs of the inmates at the particular institution.

Specific populations targeted for non-residential drug abuse treatment include the following:

- Inmates with a relatively minor or low-level drug abuse impairment.
- Inmates with a drug use disorder who do not have sufficient time to complete the residential drug abuse treatment program (discussed below).
- Inmates with longer sentences who are in need of treatment and are awaiting placement in the residential program.
- Inmates identified with a drug use history who did not participate in the residential drug abuse treatment program and are preparing for community transition.
- Inmates who completed the residential drug abuse treatment program and are required to continue treatment upon their transfer to the general inmate population.

According to BOP, 8.5% of federal inmates participated in a non-residential drug abuse treatment program in FY2009.

Residential Drug Abuse Treatment (RDAP)

BOP offers residential drug abuse treatment in 61 institutions. To be eligible for residential treatment, an inmate must (1) have a verifiable and documented drug abuse problem, (2) have no serious mental impairment that would substantially interfere with or preclude full participation in the program, (3) sign an agreement acknowledging the inmate's responsibilities while participating in the program, and (4) volunteer for the program. If an inmate is housed at an institution that does not operate a RDAP, the inmate can be transferred to an institution with an RDAP.

Inmates in residential drug abuse treatment programs are housed in separate units reserved for drug abuse treatment. Residential drug abuse treatment programs last six to 12 months (a minimum of 500 hours). Inmates in the program spend half of their day in treatment and the other half in education, work skills training, and/or other inmate programs. According to BOP, 10.9% of federal inmates participated in residential drug abuse treatment in FY2009.

Community Transition Drug Abuse Treatment

Inmates who participate in the residential drug abuse treatment program must also complete a course of follow-up treatment with a community-based treatment provider when transferred to RRC. This community transition program must be completed if an inmate, who is otherwise eligible, is to receive an early release. According to BOP, 9.4% of federal inmates participated in community transition drug abuse treatment in FY2009.

RESEARCH ON THE EFFECTIVENESS OF REHABILITATIVE PROGRAMS

One researcher concluded that, in general, the body of literature on the effectiveness of rehabilitative programming suggests that inmates who participated in Adult Basic Education (ABE), GED, postsecondary education, vocational education, correctional industries, and incarceration-based drug abuse treatment programs were significantly less likely to recidivate than those who did not participate.[26]

However, in general, research on the effectiveness of rehabilitative programming has limitations, including the following:

- Lack of scientific rigor in many studies limits the possibility of determining whether improved outcomes are directly attributable to the intervention or if there are alternative explanations for the treatment's effect.
- Studies use different definitions of recidivism (i.e., rearrest, reconviction, reincarceration, technical violations of supervised release, self-reported recidivism), which can make it difficult to compare the results of one study to another.
- Studies use different follow-up periods (e.g., six months, one year, two years).
- Many studies suffer from selection bias because they do not randomly assign inmates to either the treatment or control group; rather, in many cases inmates who participate in rehabilitation programs volunteer to participate. Selection bias prevents researchers from determining whether the treatment caused the observed effects, or whether the effect was the result of differential characteristics of inmates in the treatment and control groups (i.e., inmates in the control group were more motivated to change).
- Many studies do not control for attrition from the treatment group. To determine whether the treatment is effective, it is important to compare inmates who receive the full treatment to those who drop out of treatment and those who do not receive treatment.
- Even when studies do employ rigorous methodologies (either using random assignment or controlling for difference between the treatment and control groups), they frequently cannot identify the particular aspects of programming that contributed to the outcome.
- Many studies do not carefully differentiate among the types of programs. For example, some studies might evaluate the impact of working in a correctional industry on recidivism, but many inmates may also be receiving vocational training or participating in some other training. Also, few inmates only participate in just one rehabilitative intervention while they are incarcerated.
- Some studies do not collect data on other variables that might affect the inmate's chances of recidivating or on other variables that measure the impact the intervention had on the inmate's chances of recidivating.

One analysis suggests that some of the methodological shortcomings of research in the field might affect whether a treatment program is deemed to be effective. This analysis evaluated the relationship between a study's research methodology and the likelihood that the study found a treatment effect.[27] The study found that less methodologically rigorous studies were more likely to find a treatment effect. Moreover, less-rigorous studies were more likely to report a larger effect size than more-rigorous studies. This trend held when the researchers only compared randomized studies (i.e., studies in which subjects were randomly assigned to either a treatment or control group) to the highest-quality non-randomized studies (i.e., quasi-experimental, but the researchers attempted to statistically control for difference between subjects in the treatment and control groups). The researchers also found that when they only considered the results of studies where the findings were statistically significant, less-rigorous studies were still more likely to find a positive effect. The researchers concluded that their findings suggested that a study's research design does have an impact on a finding of effectiveness and, while their results should be seen as a preliminary step in understanding how research design affects study outcomes in criminal justice, it suggests that reviews of what works in criminal justice might be biased when nonrandomized studies are included.

REHABILITATIVE NEEDS OF FEDERAL INMATES

This section of the report provides an analysis of whether the need for rehabilitative programming changed between 1997 and 2004. The analysis uses data from the Bureau of Justice Statistics' *Survey of Inmates in State and Federal Correctional Facilities* (hereafter, "survey") for 1997 and 2004 to determine whether federal inmates in 2004 were more or less likely than inmates in 1997 to have indicators of the need for rehabilitative programming.[28] The selected indicators include the following:

- Does the inmate need a GED or a high school diploma?
- Was the inmate unemployed before being incarcerated?
- Did the inmate regularly use drugs, or was the inmate using drugs before being arrested?

These variables were chosen because they provide an indication of what type of rehabilitative programming an inmate might need.

**Table 1. Indicators of Rehabilitative Need among
Federal Inmates, 1997 and 2004.**

	1997	2004
Did not have a GED or a high school diploma	26.3%	26.8%
Unemployed before being arrested	28.2%	29.9%
Regularly used drugs	57.3%	64.6%
Used drugs before being arrested	44.8%	50.5%

Source: CRS analysis of data from the 1997 and 2004 *Survey of Inmates in State and Federal Correctional Facilities.*
Note: "Regularly used drugs" is defined as using any drug once a week or more for at least a month. "Used drugs before being arrested" is defined as using any drug in the month before being arrested for the crime(s) for which the inmate was incarcerated at the time of the interview.

Data from the 1997 and 2004 surveys show that it was likely that there was increased need for drug abuse treatment programs, but the need for literacy/GED and occupational education programs along with FPI work assignments remained flat. As shown in Table 1, in both 1997 and 2004 approximately one-quarter of federal inmates reported not having a GED or a high school diploma and approximately 30% of inmates in both years reported that they were unemployed before being arrested. While there was no significant increase in the percentage of inmates who reported not having a GED or a high school diploma or being unemployed before being arrested, inmates in 2004 were significantly more likely than inmates in 1997 to report that they had regularly used drugs and that they used drugs before being arrested.

PARTICIPATION IN REHABILITATIVE PROGRAMS

This section of the report provides an analysis of whether federal inmates with rehabilitative needs are participating in rehabilitative programming. Table 2 provides data on the overall percentage of inmates who reported currently having an FPI work assignment and the percentage of inmates who reported participating in an occupational education, literacy/GED, or some type of drug abuse treatment program during their current incarceration. Overall, between 1997 and 2004 there was a significant decrease in the percentage of inmates who reported currently having an FPI work assignment. On the other hand, there was a significant increase in the percentage of inmates who reported participating in a drug education program. There was no significant increase or decrease in the percentage of inmates who reported participating in any of the other rehabilitative programs.

The analysis used logistic regression to test whether inmates with rehabilitative needs were more likely than other inmates to participate in rehabilitative programming (see the Appendix). The results of the analysis suggest that in both 1997 and 2004, inmates who reported being unemployed before being arrested were *not* significantly more likely than other inmates to report that they had an FPI work assignment; however, in both years inmates who reported being unemployed before being arrested were significantly *less* likely than other inmates to have participated in an occupational education program. In addition, in both 1997 and 2004 inmates who reported not having a GED or a high school diploma were significantly more likely than other inmates to report that they participated in a literacy/GED program. Also, in both years inmates who reported either regular drug use or using drugs before being arrested were significantly more likely than other inmates to have participated in residential and non-residential drug abuse treatment and a drug abuse education course. Yet, the analysis also suggests that there was not a significant difference in the likelihood that inmates in 1997 and 2004 with rehabilitative needs participated in programming. This could suggest that BOP was not able to expand opportunities for rehabilitative programming between 1997 and 2004 or that inmates' desires to participate in rehabilitative programming did not increase between 1997 and 2004.

Even though inmates with rehabilitative needs were, in most cases, more likely than inmates without a need to participate in rehabilitative programs, the analysis suggests that it was less than certain that inmates with rehabilitative needs participated in programs to address their needs. The results of the analysis suggest that the probability that a typical inmate[29] with a rehabilitative need participated in a program to address that need was, in most cases, less than 1 in 2. For example, the estimated probability that a typical inmate who was unemployed before being arrested had an FPI work assignment was about 1 in 5 for both 1997 and 2004, and the probability that a typical inmate who was unemployed before being arrested participated in an occupational education course was about 2 in 5 for both years. In addition, the estimated probability that a typical inmate who either reported regular drug use or used drugs before being arrested participated in residential or non-residential drug abuse treatment in 1997 or 2004 was about 1 in 10. The estimated probability that a typical inmate who either reported regular drug use or used drugs before being arrested participated in a drug abuse education course was approximately 1 in 5 in 1997 and 3 in 10 in 2004. The results of the analysis suggest that a typical inmate without either a GED or a high school diploma was more likely than not (an approximately 1 in 2 chance in 1997 and a 3 in 5 chance in 2004) to have participated in a literacy/GED course.

Table 2. Participation in Rehabilitative Programs, 1997 and 2004.

	1997	2004
FPI work assignment	17.5%	12.0%
Occupational education	28.7%	31.7%
Literacy/GED program	24.0%	25.1%
Residential drug abuse treatment	7.2%	5.6%
Non-residential drug abuse treatment	3.8%	4.9%
Drug education program	16.7%	20.6%

Source: CRS analysis of data from the 1997 and 2004 *Survey of Inmates in State and Federal Correctional Facilities.*

The results of the analysis also suggest that the probability that the highest-participating inmates participated in rehabilitative programs was 3 in 5 or lower. For example, the probability that the highest-participating inmates who reported being unemployed before being arrested had an FPI work assignment in 1997 was approximately 3 in 5, while in 2004 it was approximately 3 in 10. Moreover, the probability that the highest-participating inmates who reported being unemployed before being arrested participated in an occupational education course was approximately 1 in 2 in 1997 and approximately 3 in 5 in 2004. The estimated probability that the highest participating inmates who reported either regular drug use or using drugs before being arrested participated in a residential drug abuse program was approximately 3 in 10 in 1997 and 2 in 5 in 2004, while the estimated probability that these inmates participated in a non-residential drug abuse program was approximately 1 in 5 in 1997 and 3 in 10 in 2004. The analysis suggests that the probability that the highest-participating inmates who reported either regularly using drugs or using drugs before being arrested participated in a drug abuse education course was approximately 1 in 2 in both

1997 and 2004. Also, the results of the analysis suggest that the probability that the highest-participating inmates who reported not having a GED or a high school diploma participated in a literacy/GED program was approximately 3 in 5 in both 1997 and 2004.

Table 3. Percentage of Inmates that Participated in BOP Rehabilitative Programs, FY2000-FY2009.

| FY | FPI Work Assignment | Education Programs | | Drug Abuse Treatment Programs | | | |
		Literacy/ GED	Occupational Education	Drug Abuse Education Course	Non-residential	Residential	Community Transition
2000	17.3%	N.A.	N.A.	12.5%	6.3%	10.0%	6.7%
2001	17.3%	N.A.	N.A.	13.2%	8.3%	11.8%	8.7%
2002	15.6%	N.A.	N.A.	13.0%	8.4%	11.8%	9.5%
2003	13.9%	14.2%	6.8%	14.3%	8.2%	12.0%	10.3%
2004	12.7%	14.5%	6.9%	14.5%	8.5%	12.0%	10.8%
2005	12.4%	14.2%	6.2%	14.3%	8.9%	11.3%	10.3%
2006	13.0%	13.8%	6.1%	14.2%	8.4%	10.7%	9.5%
2007	13.8%	12.7%	6.4%	14.1%	8.6%	10.5%	9.2%
2008	13.2%	12.5%	6.7%	14.0%	8.6%	10.6%	9.3%
2009	11.0%	12.5%	6.5%	17.8%	8.5%	10.9%	9.4%

Source: CRS presentation of data provided by U.S. Department of Justice, Bureau of Prisons.

Note: BOP was not able to provide data on the number of inmates that participated in the GED/Literacy and Occupational Training programs prior to FY2003. Percentages were calculated as the number of inmates that participated in the program divided by the *institutional* population for that fiscal year.

One shortcoming of the analysis is the age of the data used to estimate whether inmates with rehabilitative needs are participating in programs to address their needs. As noted above, the most recent data are from 2004, which is more than six years old. Could the probability of participation in rehabilitative programming have increased since the last survey was conducted? Data from BOP on the percentage of inmates who participated in rehabilitative programming each fiscal year suggest that this might not be the case. As shown in Table 3, the total proportion of federal inmates who participated in rehabilitative programming each fiscal year since FY2000 has remained relatively steady, with the exception of the proportion of inmates who had a FPI work assignment, which decreased between FY2000 and FY2009. Hence, unless inmates with rehabilitative needs accounted for a greater share of the inmates who participated in rehabilitative programming after FY2004, the data from BOP suggest that the trends observed in the 1997 and 2004 survey data could be applicable to current federal inmates.

SELECT ISSUES FOR CONGRESS

The analysis above suggests either that BOP is not offering rehabilitative programming to all inmates with a need for it, or that inmates are choosing not to participate in rehabilitative programming even though they indicate a need for it. There may be multiple explanations for both findings. Moreover, as discussed earlier, there is not necessarily conclusive evidence that rehabilitative programs for inmates are effective. This section of the report discusses two potential issues Congress might choose to consider.

Providing Access to Rehabilitative Programming

A potential issue for Congress is whether BOP has the resources it needs to carry out its mission to provide rehabilitative programming to federal inmates. According to BOP, its biggest challenge is "managing the ever increasing federal inmate population, and providing for their care and safety, as well as the safety of BOP staff and surrounding communities, within budgeted levels."[30] In its FY2011 congressional budget submission, BOP notes that it has "stretched resources, streamlined operations, improved program efficiencies, and reduced costs to operate as efficiently and effectively as possible."[31] Even though total appropriations for BOP increased every fiscal year since FY2000, BOP has dedicated a growing percentage of its base budget to cover mandatory requirements, including inmate medical care, food, utilities, fuel, and correctional staffing. BOP also reports that the inmate-to-staff ratio, which includes staff to provide rehabilitative programming, has increased over the past several fiscal years.[32] Data provided by BOP indicate that the total number of BOP staff per 1,000 inmates decreased from 242.0 in FY2000 to 202.5 in FY2009. In addition, the number of education staff per 1,000 inmates decreased from 6.8 to 5.8 between FY2000 and FY2009, and the number of psychological services staff per 1,000 inmates (which includes staff to provide drug abuse treatment) decreased from 6.4 to 5.7 over the same time period. As Congress continues its oversight of BOP, it might consider whether staffing levels at BOP are adequate to allow BOP to carry out its mission to rehabilitate inmates.

A related issue is whether BOP has enough facilities to manage the federal prison population. BOP opened 48 new prisons between FY1991 and FY2010 and additional prisons mean more classrooms and factories in which BOP can offer rehabilitative programs. In addition to providing more classrooms and factories, additional prisons decrease crowding. Less crowding could increase inmates' access to rehabilitative programming by decreasing the amount of time inmates have to wait for admission into programs. However, crowding in BOP institutions averaged 36% each fiscal year between FY2005 and FY2010. During this time period, BOP had no net increase in prison facilities.[33] BOP plans to add nearly 15,000 new bedspaces to its current capacity between FY2011 and FY2016, but even with the additional capacity BOP still projects prison crowding to increase.[34] Congress might consider whether to increase funding to BOP so it might expand its capacity and reduce crowding. Congress might also consider whether BOP should place more low, and possibly medium, security offenders in privately operated prisons.

Incentives for Participating in Rehabilitative Programs

Another potential issue before Congress is the structure of incentives for inmates to participate in rehabilitative programs. The Comprehensive Crime Control Act of 1984 (P.L. 98-473) abolished parole for federal inmates and modified how much good time credit an inmate could earn.[35] There was not a single event that led Congress to abolish parole for federal offenders; rather, it was the culmination of several critiques and concerns about sentencing policy that began in the 1970s.[36] Some viewed the discretion exercised by the judiciary and parole boards over the length of an offender's sentence as arbitrary and unfair.[37] Others thought that allowing parole boards to determine when an inmate could be released based on the inmate's behavior while incarcerated along with the goal of rehabilitation was tantamount to coddling criminals.[38] In the late 1970s, states, and eventually the federal government, started to limit judicial discretion by replacing indeterminate sentences with determinate sentences (e.g., sentencing guidelines).[39] There was also a movement to limit judicial and parole board discretion by enacting "truth-in-sentencing" laws, which required offenders sentenced for certain crimes (usually violent crimes) to serve no less than 85% of their sentence before being eligible for release.[40]

By eliminating parole and modifying the amount of good time credit an inmate could earn, Congress decreased some of the incentives inmates had to participate in rehabilitative programs. Prior to the act, when considering whether to grant an inmate parole the U.S. Parole Board considered whether an inmate had followed institutional rules while incarcerated and whether, in light of the nature and circumstances of the offense and the history and characteristics of the inmate, granting parole would depreciate the seriousness of the offense and promote disrespect of the law and jeopardize public welfare.[41] As such, inmates had an incentive to participate in rehabilitative programs in order to prove to the parole board that they would not be a threat to the community if paroled and that they had attempted to atone for their crimes. In addition, prior to the act inmates could earn up to three days of industrial good time credit per month for the first year of participation in an FPI program and up to five days of industrial good time credit per month for any succeeding year.[42] The law also permitted BOP to award the same amount of industrial good time credit to "prisoner[s] performing exceptionally meritorious service or performing duties of outstanding importance in connection with institutional operations."[43] Industrial good time credit was in addition to good time credit inmates could earn for following the institution's rules.[44] The previous good time credit system provided an incentive for inmates to participate in work programs by allowing them to earn up to an additional 36 days of industrial good time credit in the first year and up to 60 days of industrial good time credit for each additional year.

The current good time credit structure only provides inmates with an incentive to participate in basic education programs and drug abuse treatment. Under current law, inmates are not eligible for their full allotment of good time credit if it is determined that they are not making satisfactory progress on earning a high school diploma or a GED.[45] However, even if an inmate earns the full allotment of good time credit, the inmate will serve about 85% of the imposed sentence, which in most cases would be longer than the amount of time an inmate would serve under the previous system. In addition to the amount of good time credit an inmate can earn, BOP is allowed to reduce a nonviolent inmate's sentence by up to one year if the inmate participates in residential substance abuse treatment.[46] Policymakers could consider whether providing additional good time credit or longer placement in a RRC might encourage more inmates to participate in rehabilitative programs.[47] For example, current law could be amended to allow inmates who earn a vocational degree to receive additional good time credit. On the other hand, providing additional good time credit for inmates to participate in rehabilitative programming might also provide an incentive for inmates to participate for the sole purpose of reducing the time they have to serve in prison rather than participating because they wish to prepare themselves for reentry into the community. This might mean that inmates who would benefit from participating in rehabilitative programming would not be able to due to resource restrictions. In addition, it might also mean that inmates who are not fully rehabilitated would be released from prison earlier than they otherwise would have been.

APPENDIX. METHODOLOGY

This appendix provides an overview of the data used, methods used, and results of the analysis CRS conducted for this report.

Dataset

The analysis was conducted using data from the 1997 and 2004 editions of the Bureau of Justice Statistics' (BJS 's) *Survey of Inmates in State and Federal Correctional Facilities* (hereafter referred to as "the survey"). The survey provides nationally representative data on inmates held in state and federal prisons. The survey collects data on inmates' current offense and sentence; criminal history; family background and personal characteristics; prior drug and alcohol use and treatment programs; gun possession and use; and prison activities, programs, and services. Interviews for the 1997 survey were conducted between June and October of 1997 while interviews for the 2004 survey were conducted between October 2003 and May 2004.

The survey sample was selected using a two-stage stratified sampling design. A sample of federal prisons was chosen in the first stage of sampling. In 1997, one male and two female prisons were selected with certainty, while in 2004 one female and two male prisons were selected with certainty. The remaining male prisons were grouped into five strata based on the prison's security level (administrative, high, medium, low, and minimum), while the remaining female prisons were grouped into two strata (minimum and all other security levels). Within each stratum, facilities were ordered by the size of the prison's population, and a sample was selected with probability proportional to size. For the 1997 survey, 32 out of 113 male prisons and eight out of 22 female prisons were selected. For the 2004 survey, 32 out of 131 male prisons and eight out of 17 female prisons were selected.

In the second stage of sampling, a sample of inmates was selected from the prisons selected in the first stage of sampling. BOP generated a list of inmates held in the sampled prisons, and inmates were selected from the list by using a randomly selected starting point and a predetermined skip interval. However, because drug offenders are overrepresented in the federal prison population, a systematic sample would have resulted in too few non-drug offenders; hence, the federal prison population was initially oversampled so that enough non-drug offenders in the sample could be analyzed. From the initial list of inmates, one out of every three drug offenders, along with all selected non-drug offenders, were retained for the final sample. For the 1997 survey, a total of 4,479 inmates were selected for inclusion in the sample, of which 4,041 were interviewed (a 90.2% response rate). For the 2004 survey, a total of 4,253 inmates were selected for inclusion in the sample, of which 3,686 were interviewed (a 86.7% response rate). The 4,041 inmates interviewed in 1997 represented 89,072 federal inmates, while the 3,686 inmates interviewed in 2004 represented 129,299 federal inmates.

The survey data are available for download from the Inter-university Consortium for Political and Social Research's website (http://www.icpsr. umich.edu/icpsrweb/ICP SR/). However, certain variables are redacted from the publicly available dataset to protect the privacy of inmates who responded to the survey.

Two of the redacted variables—the variables that identified which strata and prison each inmate in the sample was in—were needed to adjust estimated standard errors to compensate for the complex sample design. As such, CRS had to enter into a restricted data use agreement with the National Archive of Criminal Justice Data (NACJD) in order to gain access to the redacted variables. Per the agreement with the NACJD, the restricted dataset was destroyed after this report was completed. A copy of the restricted data use agreement is on file with the author.

Methods

Logistic regression models were used to test the relationship between six dependent variables— whether the inmate had

(1) an FPI work assignment at the time of the interview,

(2) participated in a VoTech program,

(3) participated in a literacy or GED course,

(4) participated in the residential drug abuse treatment program,

(5) participated in the non-residential drug abuse treatment program, and

(6) participated in the drug abuse education course—

and the four indicators of rehabilitative need:

(1) not possessing a GED or a high school diploma,

(2) being unemployed before being arrested,

(3) using drugs regularly, and

(4) using drugs before being arrested.

Each model includes a series of demographic variables to control for any differences in program participation rates that may exist between different groups of inmates. All variables included in the analysis are dummy coded. All models were estimated using the SURVEYLOGISTIC procedure in SAS 9.2. The SUVEYLOGISTIC procedure includes variables that SAS can use to adjust standard errors to account for the complex sampling design (see description above).

The analysis excludes inmates who were held in prison but not incarcerated (i.e., pre-trial inmates) because these inmates are not cleared by BOP to participate in rehabilitative programs.

Missing data were first "logically" imputed by reviewing the survey instrument to see if data were missing because the inmate was not asked the question due to the skip pattern in the instrument. For example, data might be missing from the questions asking about whether the inmate used drugs before being arrested because in a previous series of questions the inmate responded that he or she has not used drugs. In these instances, the missing values could be replaced with "no." Data that could not be logically imputed was imputed using the MI procedure in SAS 9.2.

Each model was estimated using the 1997 data and the 2004 data. The models estimated using the 1997 data are presented in Table A-1 and the models estimated using the 2004 data are presented in Table A-2. Significance tests of the difference between coefficients estimated using each set of data were conducted using the methods specified in Raymond Paternoster et al. 's 1998 article.[48] The estimated effect that a variable had on the probability that an inmate reported participating in a rehabilitative program was calculated using the formula specified by Paul Allison.[49]

The following formula, along with the estimated coefficients presented in Table A-1 and Table A-2, can be used to calculate the probability that inmates in a particular group participated in rehabilitative programming. The formula allows the reader to compare the probability that inmates in different groups within the same year or inmates in the same group between the years participated in rehabilitative programming.

$$P = \frac{e^{\alpha + \beta_1 x_1 + \beta_2 x_2 + \ldots \beta_k x_k}}{1 + e^{\alpha + \beta_1 x_1 + \beta_2 x_2 + \ldots \beta_k x_k}}$$

Where "α" is the intercept of the estimated logistic regression model, "β" is the estimated coefficient, "x" is the value for the independent variable, and "e" is base e (roughly equal to 2.718).

Table A-1. Estimated Logistic Regression Models Using Data from the 1997 Survey.

		FPI Work Assignment	Occupational Education	Literacy/GED Program	Residential Drug Abuse Treatment	Non-residential Drug Abuse Treatment	Drug Abuse Education Course	Residential Drug Abuse Treatment	Non-residential Drug Abuse Treatment	Drug Abuse Education Course
Ages 31-40[a]	β	0.1602	0.0721	-0.0858	0.2773[n]	0.4194	0.1448	0.3452[l]	0.4927[n]	0.2007[n]
	SE	(0.1213)	(0.1099)	(0.0984)	(0.1297)	(0.2234)	(0.0977)	(0.1278)	(0.2231)	(0.0920)
Ages 41-50[a]	β	0.3419[m]	-0.1670	-0.1296	0.2160	0.1446	0.0118	0.3023	0.2104	0.0744
	SE	(0.1226)	(0.1171)	(0.0967)	(0.1580)	(0.2769)	(0.1464)	(0.1572)	(0.2763)	(0.1409)
Ages 51 or older[a]	β	0.5014[l]	-0.6092[l]	-0.1794	-0.0362	0.3273	-0.5610[m]	-0.0393	0.3288	-0.5532[m]
	SE	(0.1517)	(0.1487)	(0.1084)	(0.2968)	(0.3334)	(0.1689)	(0.2711)	(0.3261)	(0.1725)
Black[b]	β	0.3093[m]	0.3763[l]	0.2624[n]	-0.3247[n]	0.0092	-0.4045[l]	-0.3029[n]	0.0275	-0.3889[l]
	SE	(0.0936)	(0.0810)	(0.1162)	(0.1332)	(0.1633)	(0.0982)	(0.1324)	(0.1631)	(0.0961)
Hispanic[b]	β	0.2159	0.3803[l]	0.3698[m]	-0.1893	-0.0853	-0.7254[l]	-0.1993	-0.1129	-0.7370[l]
	SE	(0.1215)	(0.0882)	(0.1328)	(0.1818)	(0.2530)	(0.1781)	(0.1837)	(0.2492)	(0.1723)
Other race[b]	β	0.0787	0.2312	0.1411	-0.1807	-0.5743	-0.5490[l]	-0.1849	-0.5870	-0.5522[m]
	SE	(0.1337)	(0.1516)	(0.2259)	(0.2053)	(0.3941)	(0.1614)	(0.2161)	(0.3941)	(0.1716)
Violent offense[c]	β	1.1544[l]	0.7700[l]	0.6233[l]	0.4239[n]	0.4415[n]	0.8580[l]	0.5049[m]	0.5064[m]	0.9062[l]
	SE	(0.1389)	(0.1077)	(0.1577)	(0.1808)	(0.1998)	(0.1428)	(0.1843)	(0.1930)	(0.1427)
Drug offense[c]	β	0.5801[l]	0.6148[l]	0.7141[l]	0.5070[l]	-0.2079	0.8610[l]	0.5551[n]	-0.1633	0.8835[l]
	SE	(0.1514)	(0.0904)	(0.1542)	(0.2298)	(0.2724)	(0.1192)	(0.2366)	(0.2705)	(0.1210)
Public order offense[c]	β	0.5469[l]	0.4255[l]	0.3661[n]	0.2095	-0.2881	0.5917[l]	0.2886	-0.2292	0.6427[l]
	SE	(0.1406)	(0.0868)	(0.1647)	(0.1715)	(0.2278)	(0.1390)	(0.1743)	(0.2277)	(0.1403)

		FPI Work Assignment	Occupational Education	Literacy/GED Program	Residential Drug Abuse Treatment	Non-residential Drug Abuse Treatment	Drug Abuse Education Course	Residential Drug Abuse Treatment	Non-residential Drug Abuse Treatment	Drug Abuse Education Course
							Dependent Variables			
Non-U.S. citizen[d]	β	0.7697[l]	-0.1085	0.0658	-0.2356	-1.9892[m]	0.1687	-0.3312	-2.0569[m]	0.0950
	SE	(0.0899)	(0.1135)	(0.1480)	(0.3766)	(0.6239)	(0.2025)	(0.3648)	(0.6392)	(0.1892)
Female[e]	β	-0.1803	0.2815[m]	0.2274	0.2035	0.5593[n]	0.0249	0.1926	0.5598[n]	0.0216
	SE	(0.2017)	(0.1025)	(0.1567)	(0.2174)	(0.2747)	(0.1520)	(0.2115)	(0.2757)	(0.1476)
Recidivist[f]	β	0.1080	0.1440	0.1416	0.2667	0.4162[n]	0.1676	0.3465	0.4933[n]	0.2324[n]
	SE	(0.0926)	(0.0964)	(0.1109)	(0.1811)	(0.1957)	(0.1136)	(0.1898)	(0.2051)	(0.1102)
One year or less to serve[g]	β	-0.6422[l]	-0.1270	-0.0989	0.8002[l]	-0.1189	0.3823[m]	0.8074[l]	-0.1234	0.3849[l]
	SE	(0.1498)	(0.1131)	(0.1078)	(0.1927)	(0.1369)	(0.1158)	(0.1888)	(0.1423)	(0.1151)
Unemployed before arrest[h]	β	0.0561	-0.2770[m]	—	—	—	—	—	—	—
	SE	(0.0843)	(0.0905)							
No GED or high school diploma[i]	β	-0.3996[m]	-0.7761[l]	1.6651[l]	—	—	1.0454[l]	—	—	—
	SE	(0.1207)	(0.0986)	(0.0910)			(0.0979)			
Regularly used drugs[j]	β	—	—	—	1.4804[l]	1.1067[l]	—	—	—	—
	SE				(0.2038)	(0.2024)				
Used drugs before arrest[k]	β	—	—	—	—	—	—	1.1348[l]	0.8546[l]	0.8596[l]
	SE							(0.1591)	(0.1717)	(0.0917)
Intercept	β	-2.5573[l]	-1.4649[l]	-2.5739[l]	-4.4760[l]	-4.3257[l]	-2.9922[l]	-4.2090[l]	-4.1595[l]	-2.8477[l]
	SE	(0.2136)	(0.1870)	(0.1930)	(0.3108)	(0.3223)	(0.1818)	(0.2366)	(0.2841)	(0.1776)

Source: CRS presentation of results of analysis conducted using data from the 1997 Survey of Inmates in State and Federal Correctional Facilities.

a. Reference group is inmates between the ages of 18 and 30.
b. Reference group is white inmates.

c. Reference group is inmates convicted of property offenses.
d. Reference group is inmates who are U.S. citizens.
e. Reference group is male inmates.
f. Reference group is inmates who do not have a prior conviction.
g. Reference group is inmates who have more than a year left on their sentences.
h. Reference group is inmates who were employed before being arrested.
i. Reference group is inmates who have a GED or a high school diploma.
j. Reference group is inmates who reported that they did not regularly use drugs.
k. Reference group is inmates who reported that they were not using drugs before being arrested.
l. Significant at the p < 0.001 level.
m. Significant at the p < 0.01 level.
n. Significant at the p < 0.05 level.

Table A-2. Estimated Logistic Regression Models Using Data from the 2004 Survey.

		Dependent Variables								
		FPI Work Assignment	Occupational Education	Literacy/ GED Program	Residential Drug Abuse Treatment	Non-residential Drug Abuse Treatment	Drug Abuse Education Course	Residential Drug Abuse Treatment	Non-residential Drug Abuse Treatment	Drug Abuse Education Course
Ages 31-40[a]	β	0.3493[n]	0.1182	-0.0235	0.3601[n]	0.0728	-0.0828	0.3667[n]	0.0670	-0.0759
	SE	(0.1650)	(0.1027)	(0.0960)	(0.1764)	(0.1964)	(0.1140)	(0.1794)	(0.1966)	(0.1144)
Ages 41-50[a]	β	0.3454[m]	-0.1305	-0.0876	0.2225	0.5678[m]	-0.0007	0.2465	0.5738[m]	0.0161
	SE	(0.1474)	(0.1166)	(0.1295)	(0.1778)	(0.2043)	(0.1179)	(0.1874)	(0.2044)	(0.1150)

Dependent Variables

		FPI Work Assignment	Occupational Education	Literacy/ GED Program	Residential Drug Abuse Treatment	Non-residential Drug Abuse Treatment	Drug Abuse Education Course	Residential Drug Abuse Treatment	Non-residential Drug Abuse Treatment	Drug Abuse Education Course
Ages 51 or older[a]	β	0.0053	-0.4853[l]	-0.7122[l]	-0.0433	0.2227	-0.2835	-0.0562	0.1095	-0.3212[n]
	SE	(0.1808)	(0.1283)	(0.1159)	(0.2847)	(0.3622)	(0.1558)	(0.3002)	(0.3786)	(0.1594)
Black[b]	β	0.3247[n]	0.5541[l]	0.4393[m]	-0.3677	-0.3934	-0.0884	-0.3703	-0.4389	-0.1134
	SE	(0.1532)	(0.0848)	(0.1381)	(0.1877)	(0.2219)	(0.1118)	(0.1988)	(0.2324)	(0.1147)
Hispanic[b]	β	0.0559	0.3260[m]	0.4773[m]	-0.1406	-0.9417[m]	-0.2183	-0.1757	-1.0189[m]	-0.2624
	SE	(0.1821)	(0.1138)	(0.1785)	(0.2481)	(0.3447)	(0.1439)	(0.2553)	(0.3537)	(0.1417)
Other race[b]	β	0.3039	0.0767	0.2116	0.4252	-0.2294	0.1236	0.4025	-0.2790	0.1089
	SE	(0.2324)	(0.2124)	(0.2221)	(0.2265)	(0.2954)	(0.2014)	(0.2092)	(0.2962)	(0.1919)
Violent offense[c]	β	1.0947[l]	0.4743[m]	0.6028[l]	-0.3978	0.6135[n]	0.3421	-0.3587	0.7257[m]	0.3715
	SE	(0.2494)	(0.1612)	(0.1298)	(0.2875)	(0.2798)	(0.2024)	(0.2748)	(0.2615)	(0.1952)
Drug offense[c]	β	0.5927[m]	0.2611	0.6221[l]	0.3585	0.1338	0.4573[n]	0.3543	0.2545	0.4824[m]
	SE	(0.2470)	(0.1503)	(0.1352)	(0.2707)	(0.2338)	(0.1903)	(0.2708)	(0.2152)	(0.1775)
Public order offense[c]	β	0.5955[m]	0.2060	0.3569n	0.3336	0.2136	0.0323	0.3705	0.3174	0.0717
	SE	(0.2407)	(0.1597)	(0.1612)	(0.2348)	(0.3439)	(0.1815)	(0.2381)	(0.3250)	(0.1785)
Non-U.S. citizen[d]	β	-0.1550	-0.5500[l]	-0.3743[n]	-1.3239[l]	-0.0458	-0.6804[m]	-1.3031[l]	-0.1577	-0.7146[m]
	SE	(0.2004)	(0.1418)	(0.1456)	(0.2735)	(0.3874)	(0.2354)	(0.2770)	(0.3656)	(0.2344)
Female[e]	β	-0.1227	0.2946[n]	-0.1507	0.3094	0.2787	-0.1409	0.2686	0.2353	-0.1739
	SE	(0.2245)	(0.1366)	(0.1169)	(0.2176)	(0.1569)	(0.189)	(0.2129)	(0.1545)	(0.1214)
Recidivist[f]	β	-0.0883	0.0837	0.2120[n]	0.1146	0.5400[m]	0.4432[l]	0.1657	0.6629[l]	0.5044[l]
	SE	(0.1102)	(0.0613)	(0.0958)	(0.1745)	(0.1829)	(0.1084)	(0.1847)	(0.1868)	(0.1072)

Table A.2. (Continued)

		FPI Work Assignment	Occupational Education	Literacy/ GED Program	Residential Drug Abuse Treatment	Non-residential Drug Abuse Treatment	Drug Abuse Education Course	Residential Drug Abuse Treatment	Non-residential Drug Abuse Treatment	Drug Abuse Education Course
						Dependent Variables				
One year or less to serve[g]	β	-0.5526[l]	-0.1287	0.0169	1.3365[l]	0.3612	0.5239[l]	1.3458[l]	0.3686[n]	0.5300[l]
	SE	(0.1313)	(0.0902)	(0.1248)	(0.1658)	(0.1894)	(0.1229)	(0.1610)	(0.1850)	(0.1213)
Unemployed before arrest[h]	β	0.0970	-0.2617[m]	—	—	—	—	—	—	—
	SE	(0.1433)	(0.0884)							
No GED or high school diploma[i]	β	-0.7189[l]	-0.7027[l]	1.6926[l]	—	—	—	—	—	—
	SE	(0.1509)	(0.1078)	(0.0990)						
Regularly used drugs[j]	β	—	—	—	1.7581[l]	1.6516[l]	1.048[l]	—	—	—
	SE				(0.3266)	(0.2819)	(0.1236)			
Used drugs before arrest[k]	β	—	—	—	—	—	—	1.3403[l]	0.8138[l]	0.7839[l]
	SE							(0.1967)	(0.1786)	(0.1169)
Intercept	β	-2.6937[l]	-1.0386[l]	-2.5174[l]	-5.0617[l]	-4.9097[l]	-2.6782[l]	-4.5737[l]	-4.2230[l]	-2.4009[l]
	SE	(0.2802)	(0.2017)	(0.1857)	(0.3766)	(0.4125)	(0.2474)	(0.2640)	(0.4078)	(0.2431)

Source: CRS presentation of results of analysis conducted using data from the 2004 *Survey of Inmates in State and Federal Correctional Facilities.*

a. Reference group is inmates between the ages of 18 and 30.
b. Reference group is white inmates.
c. Reference group is inmates convicted of property offenses.
d. Reference group is inmates who are U.S. citizens.

e. Reference group is male inmates.

f. Reference group is inmates who do not have a prior conviction.

g. Reference group is inmates who have more than a year left on their sentences.

h. Reference group is inmates who were employed before being arrested.

i. Reference group is inmates who have a GED or a high school diploma.

j, Reference group is inmates who reported that they did not regularly use drugs.

k. Reference group is inmates who reported that they were not using drugs before being arrested.

l. Significant at the $p < 0.001$ level.

m. Significant at the $p < 0.01$ level.

n. Significant at the $p < 0.05$ level.

Limitations of the Data

The data used in this analysis represent the two most recent surveys conducted by BJS. However, even the most recent data are more than six years old. Hence, even though the data from 1997 and 2004 suggest some trends in terms of the rehabilitative needs of federal inmates and their participation in rehabilitative programming, it is possible that those trends have not continued. Because data in the survey are self-reported, there is the possibility of measurement error because interviewed inmates could provide inaccurate answers due to poor recollection or because they could choose to exaggerate or minimize their responses. Also, even though the survey provides a rich source of data on federal inmates, it did not collect data on every variable that might have been useful for this analysis. For example, the survey did not ask inmates if they were eligible for parole and the other data collected did not allow CRS to determine if a given inmate was eligible for parole. As such, the coefficients for the variables included in the model might be biased to the extent that omitted variables are correlated with the variables included in the models. Therefore, there must be some degree of caution when considering how much more likely inmates with rehabilitative needs were than other inmates to participate in rehabilitative programs. Finally, the variables "regularly used drugs" and "used drugs before arrest" are admittedly rough proxies for an actual diagnosis of drug abuse. It might well be that inmates who responded that they either regularly used drugs or that they used drugs before being arrested would not be diagnosed as a drug abuser.

ACKNOWLEDGMENTS

Chad C. Haddal, formerly with CRS; Jennifer E. Lake, Section Research Manager; and Kristin M. Finklea, Analyst in Domestic Security, peer reviewed this report. Patrick Purcell, formerly of CRS, and Gerald Mayer, Analyst in Labor Policy, provided insights and comments on the regression models.

End Notes

[1] U.S. Department of Justice, Bureau of Prisons, *Mission and Vision of the Bureau of Prisons*, http://www.bop.gov/ about/mission.jsp.
[2] Jeremy Travis, *But They All Come Back: Facing the Challenges of Prisoner Reentry* (Washington, DC: Urban Institute Press, 2005), pp. 323-352.

[3] BOP is authorized in law at Chapter 303 of Title 18 of the United States Code (18 U.S.C. § 4041 et seq.).

[4] U.S. Department of Justice, Bureau of Prisons, *About the Bureau of Prisons*, http://www.bop.gov/about/index.jsp.

[5] U.S. Department of Justice, Bureau of Prisons, *A Brief History of the Bureau of Prisons*, http://www.bop.gov/about/%20history.jsp.

[6] Ibid.

[7] Data provided by the U.S. Department of Justice, Bureau of Prisons. Data are on file with the author.

[8] U.S. Department of Justice, Bureau of Prisons, *State of the Bureau 2008*, Washington, DC, p. 2, http://www.bop.gov/ news/PDFs/sob08.pdf.

[9] U.S. Department of Justice, Bureau of Prisons, *Prison Types & General Information*, http://www.bop.gov/locations/institutions/index.jsp.

[10] U.S. Department of Justice, Bureau of Prisons, *Community Corrections*, http://www.bop.gov/locations/cc/index.jsp.

[11] Ibid.

[12] U.S. Department of Justice, Bureau of Prisons, *About the Federal Bureau of Prisons*, July 2007, http://www.bop.gov/ news/PDFs/ipaabout.pdf.

[13] For more information on FPI, see CRS Report RL32380, *Federal Prison Industries*, by Nathan James.

[14] Information in this section was obtained from U.S. Department of Justice, Bureau of Prisons, Program Statement 5251.06, *Work and Performance Pay, Inmate*, http://www.bop.gov/policy U.S. Department of Justice, Bureau of Prisons, Program Statement 8120.02, *Work Programs for Inmates—FPI*, http://www.bop.gov/policy/ progstat/8 120_002.pdf; U.S. Department of Justice, Bureau of Prisons, *Work Programs*, http://www.bop.gov/ inmatejrograms/workjrgms.jsp; U.S. Department of Justice, Bureau of Prisons, State of the Bureau 2008, http://www.bop.gov/news/PDFs/sob08.pdf; and U.S. Department of Justice, Federal Prison Industries, Inc., UNICOR Annual Report 2009, http://www.unicor.gov/information/publications/pdfs/corporate/catar2009.pdf.

[15] This report focuses on FPI work assignments because (1) they are usually considered more desirable because of the higher per-hour pay; (2) they allow inmates to learn a trade; and (3) an analysis of participation in all work programs would be invalid because all medically able inmates are required to have a prison work assignment, meaning that only a small number of inmates interviewed for the surveys did not work and the estimated coefficients in the model would be overly reliant on the characteristics of this small number of inmates.

[16] Information in this section was obtained from BOP Program Statement 5350.28, *Literacy Program (GED Standard)*, *http://www.bop.gov/policy* and an August 29, 2007, BOP briefing on BOP's education programs.

[17] See 18 U.S.C. § 3624(f)(1) and 18 U.S.C. § 3624(b)(3).

[18] Each prisoner serving a term of imprisonment of more than one year, but not prisoners serving a life sentence, can receive a good time credit of up to 54 days per year to count toward serving the sentence. The amount of the credit is subject to the determination of BOP. 18 U.S.C. § 3624(b).

[19] In some instances, inmates cannot opt out of the literacy program because they are required by statute to participate in it. According to BOP, inmates sentenced pursuant to the Youth Corrections Act and the Narcotics Addict Rehabilitation Act cannot opt out of the literacy program.

[20] Information in this section was obtained from U.S. Department of Justice, Bureau of Prisons, Program Statement 5353.01, *Occupational Education Programs*, http://www.bop.gov/policy U.S. Department of Justice, Bureau of Prisons, Program Statement 5300.21, *Education, Training and Leisure Time Program Standards*, http://www.bop.gov/policy/progstat/5300_021.pdf; and an August 29, 2007, BOP briefing on BOP's education programs.

[21] Information in this section was obtained from U.S. Department of Justice, Bureau of Prisons, Program Statement 5330.11, *Psychology Treatment* Program, http://www.bop.gov/policy U.S. Department of Justice, Bureau of Prisons, FY201 1 Congressional Budget Submission; U.S. Department of Justice, Bureau of Prisons, *Substance Abuse Treatment*, http://www.bop.gov/inmate_programs/substance.jsp; and a conversation on August 18, 2008, with U.S. Department of Justice, Bureau of Prisons, Office of Congressional Affairs.

[22] "Residential substance abuse treatment" is defined as a course of individual and group activities and treatment, lasting at least six months, in residential treatment facilities set apart from the general prison population (which may include pharmocotherapies, where appropriate) that may extend beyond the six-month period. 18 U.S.C. § 3621(e)(5)(A).

[23] "Aftercare" is defined as placement, case management, and monitoring in a community-based substance abuse treatment program when the prisoner leaves the custody of BOP. 18 U.S.C. § 362 1(e)(5)(C).

[24] An "eligible prisoner" is defined as a prisoner who is determined by BOP to have a substance abuse problem and to be willing to participate in a residential substance abuse treatment program. 18 U.S.C. § 3621(e)(5)(B).

[25] The following categories of inmates are not eligible for early release: (1) Immigration and Customs Enforcement detainees; (2) pretrial inmates; (3) contractual boarders (for example, District of Columbia, state, or military inmates); (4) inmates who have a prior felony or misdemeanor conviction for homicide, forcible rape, robbery, or aggravated assault, or child sexual abuse offenses; (5) inmates who are not eligible for participation in a community-based program as determined by the institution's warden on the basis of his or her professional discretion; or (6) inmates whose current offense is a felony. 28 C.F.R. § 550.58.

[26] Doris Layton MacKenzie, What Works in Corrections: Reducing the Criminal Activities of Offenders and Delinquents (New York: Cambridge University Press, 2006).

[27] David Weisburd, Cynthia M. Lum, and Anthony Petrosino, "Does Research Design Affect Study Outcomes in Criminal Justice," *The Annals of the American Academy of Political and Social Scientist*, vol. 578 (2001), p. 50.

[28] Even though the survey interviewed inmates held in both state and federal correctional facilities, the analysis only includes federal inmates. For more information, see the Appendix.

[29] A typical inmate is defined as an inmate who is black, is between the ages of 31 and 40, is convicted of a drug offense, is male, is a U.S. citizen, has a prior conviction, and has more than a year to serve on his sentence.

[30] U.S. Department of Justice, Bureau of Prisons, *FY2011 Performance Budget, Congressional Submission, Salaries and Expenses*, p. 5, http://www.justice.gov/jmd/2011justification/pdf/fy11-bop-se-justification

[31] Ibid., p. 1.

[32] Ibid., p. 5.

[33] BOP reported that it operated 116 prisons in FY2005. In FY2006, BOP closed four prison camps and opened two new prisons, leaving it with a total of 114 total prisons. BOP opened a new prison in each of FY2009 and FY2010, leaving it with a total of 116 prisons at the end of FY2010.

[34] U.S. Department of Justice, Bureau of Prisons, *FY2011 Performance Budget, Congressional Submission, Buildings and Facilities*, p. 2, http://www.justice.gov/jmd/2011justification/pdf/fy11-bop-bf-justification

[35] Anyone sentenced to incarceration for a federal crime committed after November 1, 1987, is not eligible for parole.

[36] Jeremy Travis, *But They All Come Back: Facing the Challenges of Prisoner Reentry* (Washington, DC: Urban Institute Press, 2005), pp. 17-20. For more information on the history of determinate and indeterminate sentencing structures, see CRS Report RL32766,

Federal Sentencing Guidelines: Background, Legal Analysis, and Policy Options, by Lisa M. Seghetti and Alison M. Smith.

[37] Ibid., p. 17.

[38] Ibid.

[39] Ibid., p. 19.

[40] Ibid.

[41] 18 U.S.C. § 4206(a), as it was in effect before being repealed by section 218(a) of P.L. 98-473.

[42] 18 U.S.C. § 4162, as it was in effect before being repealed by section 218(a) of P.L. 98-473.

[43] Ibid.

[44] Prior to the act, inmates who were sentenced to less than a life sentence and who observed institutional rules and were not subjected to punishment could earn the following amounts of good time credit: five days for each month if the inmate was sentenced to at least six months but less than a year; six days for each month if the inmate was sentenced to at least one year but less than three years; seven days for each month if the inmate was sentenced at least three years but less than five years; eight days for each month if the inmate was sentenced to at least five years but less than 10 years; and 10 days for each month if the sentence is 10 years or more. 18 U.S.C. § 4161, as it was in effect before being repealed by section 218(a) of P.L. 98-473.

[45] Currently, inmates can earn up to 54 days of good time credit for every year served. 18 U.S.C. § 3624(b)(1).

[46] 18 U.S.C. § 3621(e)(2)(B).

[47] Under 18 U.S.C. § 3624(c), inmates can, to the extent practicable, serve up to the last 12 months of their sentences in a residential reentry center (RRC).

[48] Raymond Paternoster, Robert Brame, and Paul Mazerolle et al., "Using the Correct Statistical Test for the Equality of Regression Coefficients," *Criminology*, vol. 36, no. 4 (1998), pp. 859-866.

[49] Paul D. Allison, *Logistic Regression Using the SAS System* (Cary, NC: SAS Institute Inc., 1999), p. 30.

In: Federal Prison Inmates
Editors: J. Pametto and E. Jenkins

ISBN: 978-1-61470-120-0
© 2011 Nova Science Publishers, Inc.

Chapter 3

FEDERAL PRISON INDUSTRIES

Nathan James

SUMMARY

UNICOR, the trade name for Federal Prison Industries, Inc. (FPI), is a government-owned corporation that employs offenders incarcerated in correctional facilities under the Federal Bureau of Prisons (BOP). UNICOR manufactures products and provides services that are sold to executive agencies in the federal government. FPI was created to serve as a means for managing, training, and rehabilitating inmates in the federal prison system through employment in one of its industries.

By statute, UNICOR must be economically self-sustaining, thus it does not receive funding through congressional appropriations. In FY2009, FPI generated $885.3 million in sales. UNICOR uses the revenue it generates to purchase raw material and equipment; pay wages to inmates and staff; and invest in expansion of its facilities. Of the revenues generated by FPI's products and services, approximately 80% go toward the purchase of raw material and equipment; 17% go toward staff salaries; and 4% go toward inmate salaries.

Although there have been many studies on the recidivism rate and societal factors that may contribute to it, there are only a handful of rigorous evaluations of the effect that participation in correctional industries (i.e., FPI) has on recidivism. What research exists suggests that inmates who participate in correctional industries are less likely to recidivate than inmates who do not participate, but the results are not conclusive.

The previous Administration made several efforts to mitigate the competitive advantage UNICOR has over the private sector. Going beyond the previous Administration's efforts, Congress took legislative action to lessen the adverse impact FPI has caused on small businesses. For example, in 2002, 2003, and 2004, Congress passed legislation that modified FPI's mandatory source clause with respect to procurements made by the Department of Defense and the Central Intelligence Agency (CIA). In 2004, Congress passed legislation limiting funds appropriated for FY2004 to be used by federal agencies for the purchase of products or services manufactured by FPI under certain circumstances. This provision was extended permanently in FY2005. In the 110th Congress, the National Defense Authorization Act for Fiscal Year 2008 (P.L. 110-181) modified the way in which DOD procures products from FPI.

There are several issues Congress might consider as it continues its oversight of FPI, including whether FPI should be involved in emerging technology markets as a way to provide inmates with more job-ready skills for post-release employment and whether FPI should be allowed to enter into partnerships with private businesses.

INTRODUCTION

UNICOR,[1] the trade name for Federal Prison Industries, Inc. (FPI), is a government-owned corporation that employs offenders incarcerated in correctional facilities under the Department of Justice's (DOJ's) Federal Bureau of Prisons (BOP).[2] UNICOR manufactures products and provides services that are sold to executive agencies in the federal government. Although UNICOR industries are located within various federal prisons, they operate independently from the prison. FPI was created to serve as a means for managing, training and rehabilitating inmates in the federal prison system through employment in one of its eight industries.

UNICOR's enabling legislation[3] and the Federal Acquisition Regulation (FAR)[4] require federal agencies to procure *products* offered by UNICOR, unless authorized by UNICOR to solicit bids from the private sector.[5] (See discussion below, under the "Legislative History" section.) Such waivers can be granted by UNICOR to executive agencies if its price exceeds the current market price for comparable products.[6] Federal agencies, however, are not required to procure *services* provided by UNICOR but are encouraged to do so pursuant to FAR.[7] It is this "mandatory source clause"[8] that has drawn controversy over the years.

This report opens with a discussion of FPI's background and a brief review of the research on whether participating in correctional industries reduces recidivism. It then summarizes the statutory history of FPI and other laws affecting the industry. The report concludes with an examination of some policy considerations relating to FPI. This report does not address the related debates on inmate labor, criminal rehabilitation, or competitive versus noncompetitive federal government contracting.

BACKGROUND

As the federal prison system was established in the first decade of the 20th century, factories were constructed within prisons to manufacture products needed by the federal government and to provide prisoners with job skills and keep them from being idle. Labor organizations, however, had been making arguments against prison industries since the late 1 800s due to the poor conditions in which inmates were working and their perception that the industries were taking jobs away from law abiding citizens. The Depression of the 1930s and the resulting high levels of unemployment crystalized the debate. UNICOR was established in 1934 under an executive order issued by President Franklin Delano Roosevelt.[9] The purpose of UNICOR was to consolidate the operations of all federal prison industries in order to provide training opportunities for inmates and "diversify the production of prison shops so that no individual industry would be substantially affected."[10]

Authority

FPI is administered by a six-person Board of Directors that is appointed by the President. Its enabling act[11] requires that representatives of industries, agriculture, labor, and retailers and consumers serve as board members.[12] The board's decision-making regarding products to be manufactured and areas of expansion are driven by a goal of employing the greatest possible number of inmates.[13]

Activities

UNICOR has 98 factories in federal prisons representing seven different industrial operations. UNICOR's seven industrial operations are comprised of roughly 175 different types of products and services.[14] UNICOR's industrial operations include the following:

- clothing and textiles;
- electronics;
- fleet management and vehicular components;
- industrial products;
- office furniture;
- recycling activities; and
- services (which includes data entry and encoding).[15]

UNICOR is economically self-sustaining and does not receive funding through congressional appropriations. In FY2009, FPI generated $885.3 million in sales.[16] UNICOR uses the revenue it generates to purchase raw material and equipment; pay wages to inmates and staff; and invest in expansion of its facilities. Of the revenues generated by FPI's products and services, approximately 80% go toward the purchase of raw material and equipment; 17% go toward staff salaries; and 4% go toward inmate salaries.[17] Inmates earn from $0.23 per hour up to a maximum of $1.15 per hour, depending on their proficiency and educational level, among other things. Under BOP 's Inmate Financial Responsibility Program, all inmates who have court ordered financial obligations must use at least 50% of their FPI income to satisfy those debts; the rest may be retained by the inmate.[18]

Inmate Participation in FPI

Under current law, all physically able inmates who are not a security risk are required to work.[19] Those inmates who are not employed by FPI have other labor assignments in the prison. FPI work assignments are usually considered more desirable because wages are higher and because they allow inmates to learn a trade. However, this is not to discount the importance of regular prison work assignments. Both regular and FPI work assignments can provide inmates with "soft skills" (e.g., punctuality, learning the importance of doing a job correctly, following directions from supervisors). Also, both types of work assignments can contribute to institutional order by reducing inmate idleness. Nevertheless, regular prison work assignments provide for the operation and maintenance of prison facilities, hence these work assignments will exist as long as BOP operates prisons; the availability of FPI work assignments is more volatile.

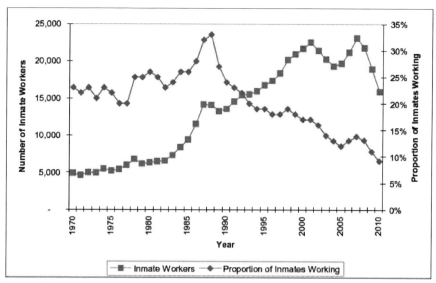

Source: CRS presentation of data provided by the U.S. Department of Justice, Bureau of Prisons.

Figure 1. Federal Inmates Employed in FPI and Proportion of Total Inmate Population Employed by FPI, 1970-2010.

Data suggest that the availability of FPI work assignments is decreasing. As shown in Figure 1, in nearly every year between 1970 and 2001, the number of inmates employed by FPI increased. Between 2001 and 2010, the number of inmates employed by FPI fluctuated between high of approximately 23,200 inmates in 2007 and a low of approximately 15,900 in 2010. However, even though the number of inmates that had an FPI work assignment has, in general, increased since 1970, the proportion of the inmate population employed by FPI has generally decreased since the late 1980s.

EFFECT OF CORRECTIONAL INDUSTRIES ON RECIDIVISM

Although there have been many studies on the recidivism rate and societal factors that may contribute to it, there are only a handful of rigorous evaluations of the effect that participation in correctional industries (i.e., FPI) has on recidivism. What research exists suggests that inmates who participate in correctional industries are less likely to recidivate than inmates who do not participate, but the results are not conclusive. This section of the report provides a brief overview of two studies that synthesized the results of evaluations of correctional industries.

A 2006 analysis of two different studies of correctional industries programs evaluated the impact of these programs on recidivism.[20] The results of the analysis indicated inmates who worked in correctional industries were less likely to recidivate than those who did not. However, the researcher concluded that given the limited number of rigorous evaluations of correctional industries programs, it was not possible to make any definitive conclusions about the ability of these programs to reduce recidivism.

Another analysis conducted in 2000 that summarized the results of four evaluations of correctional industries programs also found that inmates who participated in correctional industries programs were less likely to recidivate.[21] However, the researchers reported that they could not rule out sampling error as a possible explanation for the positive effect. The researchers also reported that many of the studies included in the analysis lacked stringent methodological rigor, thereby preventing the researchers from concluding that the programs lead directly to decreased re-offending.

ADMINISTRATIVE EFFORTS TO REFORM FPI

Over the years, critics have asserted that FPI has an unfair advantage over private business, They argue that FPI's mandatory source clause produces a monopoly-like environment that usurps and supplants the bidding process for federal contracts. FPI maintains that the mandatory source clause is paramount to keeping prison industries in operation. Furthermore, FPI asserts that the work opportunities it provides are necessary to manage and rehabilitate federal inmates. UNICOR made several efforts, however, to lessen the impact of its industries on small businesses by leveling the playing field with respect to its mandatory preference over the private sector. Efforts have also been taken to reduce FPI's reliance on its mandatory source preference.[22]

For example, in May 2003 UNICOR's Board of Directors adopted a resolution that raises the threshold for mandatory use of FPI from \$25 to \$2,500. By raising the threshold, FPI's Board of Directors in essence eliminated FPI's mandatory source clause for purchases up to \$2,500 and is now allowing federal agencies to go directly to the private sector for any purchase under \$2,500. On a related matter, FPI's Board of Directors adopted a resolution that now requires that FPI approve requests for waivers in all cases where the private sector provides a lower cost. Prior to the board's decision regarding waivers, FPI, on average, granted 87% of waivers that were requested.[23] Its Board of Directors also directed FPI to waive its mandatory source status for products where the FPI's share of the federal market is in excess of 20%. Finally, the Board of Directors requires prison-made products sold by FPI to have at least 20% of its value contributed by inmate labor.

In addition to FPI's Board of Director's decisions, federal agencies have begun to evaluate FPI's contract performance. According to testimony at a Senate hearing on FPI, "while this [the evaluation of FPI's contract performance] did not change FPI's mandatory preference status, it was an important first step in helping FPI better monitor and improve its own performance ... [which would assist] FPI as they move toward being more competitive in the federal marketplace."[24]

LEGISLATIVE HISTORY

While UNICOR was originally authorized in 1934 through P.L. 73-46 1 and Executive Order 6917, the *current* statutory authority for UNICOR was first codified in the 1948 revision of the "Crimes and Criminal procedure" statutes.[25] The only amendments to the statute were provisions added in 1988, 1990, 1992, and 2002.[26]

The question of whether UNICOR is unfairly competing with private businesses, particularly small businesses, in the federal market has been an issue of debate. In 1989, Congress considered a proposal that would have provided the private sector with greater opportunity to compete for DOD contracts. In 2002, Congress passed legislation that modified FPI's mandatory source clause with respect to the DOD,[27] see discussion below.

The absence of legislative activity on this issue for over a half century (from 1934 to 1988) is notable. However, over the past several decades, the erosion of the nation's manufacturing sector and the increase in the federal inmate population at the same time the federal government was downsizing increased congressional interest in FPI.

Only those laws that made substantial changes to the operation of FPI will be discussed below.

The Anti-Drug Abuse Act of 1988

The Anti-Drug Abuse Act of 1988 (P.L. 100-690) required that UNICOR meet specific requirements to ease the impact of its activities upon the private sector. Before approving the expansion of an existing product or the creation of a new product, the act required UNICOR to

- prepare a written analysis of the likely impact of UNICOR's expansion on industry and free labor;
- announce in an appropriate publication the plans for expansion and invite comments on the plan;
- advise affected trade associations;
- provide the UNICOR board of directors with the plans for expansion prior to the board making a decision on the expansion;
- provide opportunity to affected trade associations or relevant business representatives to comment to the Board of Directors on the proposal; and
- publish final decisions made by the Board of Directors.

The National Defense Authorization Act for FY2002

The National Defense Authorization Act for FY2002 (P.L. 107-107) required the Secretary of Defense to use competitive procedures for the procurement of the product if it is determined that the product is not comparable in price, quality and time of delivery to products available from the private sector. In doing so, the act required the Secretary of Defense to conduct research and market analysis with respect to the price, quality and time of delivery of FPI products prior to purchasing the product from FPI to determine whether the products are comparable to products from the private sector.

The Bob Stump National Defense Authorization Act for FY2003

Similar to P.L. 107-107, the Bob Stump National Defense Authorization Act for Fiscal Year 2003 (P.L. 107-314) also required the Secretary of Defense to use competitive procedures for the procurement of the product if it is determined that the product is not comparable in price, quality and time of delivery to products available from the private sector. With respect to the market research determination, the act made such determinations final and not subject to review. The act required that FPI perform its contractual obligations to the same extent as any other contractor for the DOD. It prohibits a DOD contractor or potential contractor from using FPI as a subcontractor and it also prohibits the Secretary of Defense from entering into a contract with FPI under which an inmate worker would have access to sensitive information.

The Consolidated Appropriations Act of 2004

The Consolidated Appropriations Act of 2004 (P.L. 108-199) modified FPI's mandatory source clause during FY2004 by prohibiting funds appropriated by Congress for FY2004 to be used by any federal executive agency for the purchase of products or services manufactured by FPI unless the agency making the purchase determines that the products or services are being provided at the best value, which are in line with government-wide procurement regulations.

Consolidated Appropriations Act, 2005

The Consolidated Appropriations Act, 2005 (P.L. 108-447) permanently extended the provision in the Consolidated Appropriations Act of 2004 (P.L. 108-199) related to FPI's mandatory source clause. The provision prevents federal agencies from using appropriated funds for purchasing FPI products or services unless the agency determines that the product or service provides the best value for the agency.

Intelligence Authorization Act for FY2004

The Intelligence Authorization Act for FY2004 (P.L. 108-177) required the Director of the Central Intelligence Agency to only make purchases from FPI if he determines that the product or service best meets the agency's needs.

The National Defense Authorization Act for FY2008

The National Defense Authorization Act for Fiscal Year 2008 (P.L. 110-181) amended current law to require the Secretary of Defense to do market research to determine whether an FPI product is comparable to products available from the private sector that best meet the needs of Department of Defense (DOD) in terms of price, quality, and time of delivery before purchasing a product that FPI produces in which FPI does not have a significant market share. If the Secretary determines that an FPI product is not comparable to private sector products in terms of price, quality, or time of delivery, the Secretary must then use competitive procedures for the procurement of the product, or make an individual purchase under a multiple award contract in accordance with the competition requirements applicable to such a contract. In cases where FPI is determined to have a significant market share, the Secretary of Defense can purchase a product from FPI only if the Secretary uses competitive procedures for procuring the product, or makes an individual purchase under a multiple award contract in accordance with the competition requirements applicable to such a contract.

POLICY CONSIDERATIONS

This section of the report provides an overview of some select issues Congress might consider as it continues oversight of FPI. Among the issues Congress might consider is whether FPI should be involved in emerging technology markets as a way to provide inmates with more job-ready skills for post-release employment and whether FPI should be allowed to enter into partnerships with private businesses.

Providing Inmates with Current Skills

Most of FPI's current operations are based on a manufacturing, mass-production, low-skilled labor economy of the 1930s. Inmates employed in FPI are working in "a labor-intensive manner" where the emphasis is on employing as many inmates as possible with each inmate producing little output.[28] While inmates can learn critical skills such as good workplace habits, accountability and the importance of being dependable, there is some concern about whether the trade skills inmates learn while participating in FPI are marketable after they are released. As FPI notes, the U.S. economy is changing and many jobs requiring minimal technical skills are being moved overseas.[29] According to FPI, it is exploring ways to develop more opportunities for inmates to learn skills in emerging technologies such as the environmental and alternative energy sectors.[30] Congress could consider modifying recent changes to FPI's mandatory source clause so that federal agencies would be required to purchase emerging technology products and services from FPI while continuing to require agencies to purchase other products only if the agency determines that the product provides the best value. This option may promote FPI expansion into markets that will provide some inmates with skills that are more in-tune with the economy. However, there might be some concern that FPI would gain too large of a share of the federal market, thereby pushing out private vendors.

Public-Private Partnerships for FPI

As discussed above, most federal agencies are required to procure goods from FPI, if the agency determines that the goods offered by FPI provide the best value. However, over the past decade, out of concern that FPI has an unfair advantage over private businesses when it came to procuring federal contracts, both the Administration and Congress have taken actions to limit the scope of FPI's mandatory source clause. According to FPI, the changes to the mandatory source clause are affecting FPI's ability to provide work opportunities to inmates. FPI reported that in FY2009 it downsized factories at 19 facilities because of "prior legislative changes and procurement directives, increased competitive pressures, and a soft economic climate."[31] According to BOP, in FY2000 FPI operated 103 factories.[32] The number of factories operated by FPI peaked in FY2007 at 110. In FY2009, FPI operated 98 factories. One issue Congress might consider is whether there is a way to modify FPI's mandatory source clause to allow it to provide work opportunities to federal inmates while also minimizing FPI's competition with private business.

Policymakers could consider permitting FPI to enter into public-private partnerships, such as those entered into by state correctional institutions under the Prison Industry Enhancement Certification Program (PIECP). Under PIECP, private businesses can use prison workers to make products that can be sold on the open market,[33] but the program has several conditions to protect private employees from unfair competition from incarcerated individuals.[34] Allowing FPI to enter into partnerships with private businesses to produce goods for sale on the open market might reduce some of the tension surrounding FPI's mandatory source clause and access to federal contracts for small businesses because FPI would not have to rely on sales to the federal government to provide work opportunities for inmates. In addition to potentially expanding the number of FPI work assignments available to inmates, allowing FPI to enter into a partnership with private business might enable FPI to venture into markets that it could not by working solely with the federal government. For example, FPI might become more involved in high-tech manufacturing work. This could provide inmates with opportunities to learn skills that would be more marketable after release. Partnerships with private companies may also provide inmates an opportunity to connect with companies that might employ them after they are released. Also, BOP could take deductions from higher inmate wages to help offset some of the costs of incarceration. If Congress chooses to allow FPI to enter into partnerships with private businesses, it could also consider requiring a certain percentage of inmate wages to be placed in an account that would serve as "start-up" money for the inmate after being released.

Despite some of the potential benefits that could be realized by allowing FPI to partner with private businesses, there might also be concerns about prison workers competing for jobs with non-incarcerated individuals, especially as the country is rebounding from a recession and unemployment remains comparatively high. In addition, one researcher found that there is a poor track record when it comes to private businesses partnering with correctional agencies to employ prisoners. The researcher reported that in 2002, there were 188 partnerships between state correctional agencies and private businesses, employing approximately 3,700 inmates (less than 0.3% of the prison population).[35] According to the author, few firms find it economically viable to enter into partnerships with correctional agencies because there are higher costs associated with operating a business in a prison environment and employers are required to pay inmates the prevailing wage even though they tend to be lower-skilled than the rest of the workforce.[36]

End Notes

[1] UNICOR and the FPI are used interchangeably throughout this report.

[2] This report does not cover industries in state prison, often referred to as the Private Sector/ Prison Industry Enhancement Certification (PIE) program. The PIE program was authorized by Congress in 1979 in the Justice System Improvement Act (P.L. 96-157).

[3] See 18 USC §4121 *et seq.*

[4] FAR was developed in accordance with the requirements of the Office of Federal Procurement Policy Act of 1974 (P.L. 93-400).

[5] Under current law (18 USC §4124(a)) and regulations (48 C.F.R.), federal agencies must procure products from FPI, unless granted a waiver by FPI (48 CFR 8.604), that are listed as being manufactured by UNICOR in the corporation's catalog or schedule of products.

[6] See Bureau of Prisons Program Statement 8224.02, *FPI Pricing Procedures.*

[7] FAR encourages federal agencies to treat UNICOR as a "preferential source" in the procurement of services. See 41 CFR § 101-26, 107; 48 CFR §302-5, 8.002, 8.602, 8.603, 8.605(f), and 8.704.

[8] Also referred to as "superpreference," "sole source," or "preferential status."

[9] See Executive Order 6917.

[10] Franklin Delano Roosevelt, *The Public Papers and Addresses of Franklin D. Roosevelt*, vol. 3 (New York: Random House, 1938), p. 497. These principles are reflected in the current statutory authority for FPI, see 18 USC §4122(b).

[11] See 18 USC §4121.

[12] In addition to the five board members who must be from the aforementioned groups, the Attorney General and the Secretary of Defense (or their designee) also serve as board members.

[13] Under 18 USC §4122(b)(1), this goal is explicit, along with other goals to "diversify, so far as practicable, prison industrial operations," and to "so operate the prison shops that no single private industry shall be forced to bear an undue burden of competition from the products of the prison workshops, and to reduce to a minimum competition with private industry or free labor."

[14] Federal Prison Industries, Inc., *Annual Report 2009*, http://www.unicor.gov/information/publications/pdfs/corporate/catar2009_C.pdf.

[15] Ibid.

[16] Ibid.

[17] Ibid.

[18] Ibid; John W. Roberts, *Work, Education, and Public Safety: A Brief History of Federal Prison Industries*, at http://www.unicor.gov/about/organization/history

[19] Title XXIX, §2905 of the Crime Control Act of 1990 (P.L. 10 1-647) required that all offenders in federal prisons must work (the act permitted limitations to this rule on security and health-related grounds).

[20] Doris Layton MacKenzie, What Works in Corrections: Reducing the Criminal Activities of Offenders and Delinquents (New York: Cambridge University Press, 2006), p. 102.

[21] David B. Wilson, Catherine A. Gallagher, and Doris L. MacKenzie, "A Meta-analysis of Correctional-based Education, Vocation, and Work Programs for Adult Offenders," Journal of Research in Crime and Delinquency, vol. 37 (2000), p. 356.

[22] A previous effort to eliminate FPI's mandatory source clause came during the Clinton Administration in 1993 when Vice President Al Gore recommended that the mandatory source provision be eliminated and that UNICOR be exempt from the FAR in order to better compete with the private sector in terms of delivery schedules and costs.

[23] CRS analysis of FPI waiver data from FY1994 to the first six months in FY2004.

[24] Testimony of Jack R. Williams, Jr., in U.S. Congress, Senate Committee on Governmental Affairs, Subcommittee on Financial Management, the Budget, and International Security, *Making Federal Prison Industries Subject to Competitive Bidding*, hearing on S. 346, 108th Cong., 2nd sess., April 7, 2004 (Washington: GPO, 2004).

[25] P.L. 80-772, codified at 18 USC §4121 *et seq.*

[26] The 1988 Anti-Drug Abuse Act (P.L. 100-690) authorized UNICOR to borrow from and invest in the U.S. Treasury and added *the "reasonable share" language regarding market capture*. The 1990 Crime Control Act (P.L. 101-647) required federal agencies to report information on the purchase of UNICOR products and services. The Small Business Research and Development Enhancement Act of 1992 (P.L. 102-564) modified the reporting requirements so that federal agencies provide separate reports of UNICOR purchases to the Federal Procurement Data System.

[27] See 10 USC §2410n.

[28] Statement of BOP Director Kathleen Hawk Sawyer, in U.S. Congress, House Committee on the Judiciary, *Federal Prison Industries*, hearings, 106th Cong., 2nd sess., October 5, 2000.

[29] U.S. Department of Justice, Bureau of Prisons, Federal Prison Industries, *Federal Prison Industries, Inc. Annual Report 2009*, p. 8, http://www.unicor.gov/information/publications/pdfs/corporate/catar2009.pdf.

[30] Ibid.

[31] Ibid.

[32] Data supplied by the U.S. Department of Justice, Bureau of Prisons.

[33] Prisoner-made goods produced through PIECP-certified programs are not subject to the prohibitions set forth in the Amherst-Sumners Act or the Walsh-Healey Act. The provisions of the Amherst-Sumners Act (18 U.S.C. § 1761(a)) create exemptions to federal restrictions in the marketability of prison-made goods. Generally, it is illegal for an individual to transport such goods in interstate commerce or from a foreign country. Exemptions are delineated for certain individuals on parole, probation, or supervised release. In addition, the prohibition on interstate commerce of prisoner-made goods does not apply to agricultural commodities or parts for the repair of farm machinery, nor to commodities manufactured in a federal, District of Columbia (DC), or state institution for use by the federal government, the District of Columbia, or any state or political subdivision of a state or not-for-profit organizations. The act effectively prevents most jail and prison inmates in the United States from producing goods for sale in open markets. Under the Walsh-Healey Act (41 U.S.C. §3 5), any contract made and entered into by any Executive department, independent establishment, or other agency of instrumentality of the United States, District of Columbia, or any corporation whose stock is owned by the United States for the manufacture or

furnishing of materials, supplies, articles, and equipment in any amount exceeding $10,000 is subject to certain stipulations under the act. One of these stipulations is that the contractor cannot use convict labor to manufacture, produce, or furnish any of the materials, supplies, articles, or equipment included in the contract.

[34] A PIECP-certified program must have (1) legislative authority to pay wages at a rate not less than that paid for similar work in the same locality's private sector; (2) written assurances that the program will not result in the displacement of previously employed workers; (3) authority to provide worker benefits, including workers' compensation or its equivalent; (4) authority to involve the private sector in the production and sale of prisoner-made goods; (5) written assurances that inmate participation is voluntary; (6) legislative or administrative authority to collect and provide financial contributions of not less than 5% and not more than 20% of gross wages to crime victim compensation/assistance programs and legislative or administrative authority for crime victim compensation/assistance programs to accept such financial contributions; (7) written proof of consultation with organized labor and local private industry before program startup; and (8) compliance with the National Environmental Policy Act and related federal environmental review requirements. In addition to deductions for crime victim compensation, correctional departments may take deductions for room and board, taxes (such as federal, state, FICA), and family support. Deductions cannot exceed 80% of gross wages. The Bureau of Justice Assistance (BJA) is responsible for certifying that correctional institutions are adhering to the program's requirements. For more information, see U.S. Department of Justice, Office of Justice Programs, Bureau of Justice Assistance, *Prison Industry Enhancement Certification Program*, Program Brief, NCJ 193772, July, 2002, http://www.ncjrs.gov/pdffiles1/bja/193772.pdf.

[35] Jeremy Travis, *But They All Come Back: Facing the Challenges of Prisoner Reentry* (Washington, DC: Urban Institute Press, 2005), p. 156.

[36] Ibid., pp. 156-157.

In: Federal Prison Inmates
Editors: J. Pametto and E. Jenkins

ISBN: 978-1-61470-120-0
© 2011 Nova Science Publishers, Inc.

Chapter 4

FACTORIES WITH FENCES: 75 YEARS OF CHANGING LIVES

Jennifer Pametto and Erwin Jenkins

Prison industries work programs have grown from deep-seeded roots which have withstood the challenges of time. From the late 1700s, spanning the Civil War, Great Depression, World War II and other major defense conflicts, and despite periods of criticism from detractors, increasingly constrictive procurement laws, misinformation and stigma associated with the value of inmate-made goods, prison industry work programs have endured.

IN APPRECIATION

Chief Justice Warren E. Burger

Warren E. Burger, our Nation's 15th Chief Justice, was a tireless advocate of prison reform. He believed that creating prison correctional and industrial programs to provide inmates meaningful work skills training while incarcerated, would set the course for a productive future, upon release.

Chief Justice Burger served as Co-Chairman of the National Prison Industries Task Force and was convinced that the keys to developing successful correctional programs included education, jobs training and employment. To this end, he spearheaded a series of outreach efforts including conferences, seminars and studies to extol the merits of *factories with fences.*

An adept communicator, Chief Justice Burger's campaign to educate the public gained support and sentiment for prison industry programs. Being attuned to private sector business and industry interests, he was particularly sensitive about the need to achieve balance between outside interests and correctional goals. Chief Justice Burger also inherently understood that work ethic development in inmates, would eventually lead to a reduction in recidivism.

Warren Burger's 17 year tenure as Chief Justice of the United States and his commitment to *factories with fences* have left a lasting imprint. In recognition of his vision, contributions and dedication to prison reform and prison industries programs, we proudly recognize and thank him, wholeheartedly.

> *"It makes no sense to put people in prison and not train them to do something constructive."*
> — Chief Justice Warren E. Burger

"We must accept the reality that to confine offenders behind walls without trying to change them is an expensive folly with short term benefits — winning the battles while losing the war. It is wrong. It is expensive. It is stupid."[*]

Chief Justice Warren E. Burger
1907 – 1995

---

[*] Quoted from J. Petersilia's "When Prisoners Come Home: Parole and Prisoner Reentry"; page 93

It is the mission of Federal Prison Industries, Inc. (FPI) to employ and provide job skills training to the greatest practicable number of inmates confined within the Federal Bureau of Prisons; contribute to the safety and security of our Nation's federal correctional facilities by keeping inmates constructively occupied; produce market-priced quality goods and services; operate in a self-sustaining manner; and minimize FPI's impact on private business and labor.

THE FOUNDATION OF FEDERAL PRISON INDUSTRIES, INC.

During the 1930s, the Bureau of Prisons developed four categories of inmate work assignments:

1. **Institutional:** prison operations support such as janitorial duties, grounds keeping, food preparation, clerical assistance, routine maintenance and repair work.
2. **Farming:** in that every federal prison maintained a farm, until the 1970s.
3. **Public Service:** highway construction, forestry on public lands, grounds maintenance on military bases, and assistance to other federal agencies.
4. **Prison Industries:** meaningful work in prison factories, producing goods for sale to the Federal Government.

Because none of the categories, alone, could support all inmates who needed work, the options afforded by the above work segments ensured sufficient levels of meaningful work for everyone, complete with established procedures, regular hours, and programmatic goals.

Prison Industries was the heart of the work program. It could employ a large enough percentage of the inmate population to relieve pressure from other work categories so as not to unnecessarily dilute job assignments.

By providing job skills training, Prison Industries could provide skills training which was rehabilitative, by design. It could likewise generate financial support for educational and recreational programs, pay modest inmate wages and, thereby, ease taxpayer burden.

Nevertheless, in the Bureau's early years, powerful opposition to prison industrial programs from labor unions and business interests ensued.

Inmates manufactured a variety of brushes and brooms for government agencies.

Building a Strong Foundation

Bureau of Prisons Director, Sanford Bates, and Assistant Director, James Bennett, crafted a comprehensive plan for the operation of Federal Prison Industries, Incorporated (FPI). This wholly-owned government corporation was designed so that it would not interfere significantly with private industry and involve minimal taxpayer support.

Inmates learned farming techniques while providing fresh produce for the institution.

In order to create work programs necessary for prison safety and inmate rehabilitation while avoiding the alienation of labor and business...

1. Federal Prison Industries, Inc., would make products for sale exclusively to the Federal Government; it would not compete against private sector companies in the commercial market.
2. FPI would be sufficiently diversified so as to avoid undue impact upon any particular industry. The sale of its products would be limited to the Federal Government.
   Moreover, FPI's suppliers would be private, so that its program would generate business for private companies.
3. A Board of Directors, comprised of representatives from business, labor, agriculture, consumer groups, and Government, would ensure that FPI would not cause undue hardship on any industry. Further, the Board would determine those product lines to be avoided, abolished, and those in which production should be moderated — in part, to minimize the impact of prison labor on free enterprise.
4. Industrial work would be an important rehabilitative activity by giving inmates experience in various skilled trades and teaching them *good* work habits.
5. Inmates would be paid for their labor from the corporation's revenues. Inmates could use their stipends to purchase goods from the institution commissary, to help support their families, and/or to pay fines or restitution. FPI proceeds would also be used to pay inmates in other work categories (such as farming and institutional support), albeit at lower pay scales.
6. The profits from FPI sales would be deposited to a revolving fund which would finance all industrial operations (including capital improvements) and to help subsidize other prison inmate programs. In other words, the Government got more value for its money; and that same money eventually passed back into the economy, in the form of staff salaries, inmate wages, and payments to private sector vendors.

Despite this carefully crafted plan, when legislation authorizing the creation of Federal Prison Industries, Inc., was introduced in Congress, the American Federation of Labor (AFL) immediately voiced its opposition. President Franklin D. Roosevelt took a strong, personal interest in the matter, and one rainy morning in 1934, called Director Bates and AFL President William Green to the Oval Office.

During the meeting, Bates and Roosevelt were able to draw out Green's objections to the proposed legislation, as well as his suggestions for improvement. Ultimately, the American Federation of Labor withdrew its opposition.

On June 23, 1934, President Roosevelt signed the law that authorized the establishment of Federal Prison Industries, and on December 11, 1934, he issued Executive Order 6917, which formally created Federal Prison Industries, Inc. FPI officially commenced operations on January 1, 1935.

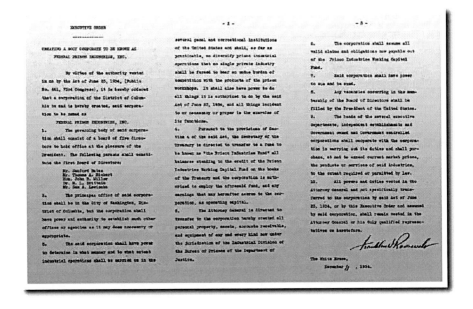

President Roosevelt's 1934 Executive Order establishing Federal Prison Industries, Inc.

A LOOK AT EARLY PRISON REFORMS

Incarceration was not championed as a more humane form of punishment until the mid 18th century. Until then, crime was looked upon as a sinful act, rather than a social problem, and "justice" was achieved by public humiliation, torture, banishment, mutilation and execution.

Jails during these times served primarily as holding cells to detain those who awaited trial, sentencing, or were unable to pay their debts.

Suffice it to say that conditions were deplorable, harboring sickness, disease and death.

Confinement was often portable in early America. Mobile holding pens could transport inmates for hard labor, as well as serve as temporary jails.

In the late 1600s, a Quaker by the name of William Penn arrived in the colony later named after him — Pennsylvania — and professed and implemented a new penal code known as the *Great Law*. In place of public humiliation and dire forms of punishment, it advocated imprisonment, hard labor, fines, and, ultimately, reform and rehabilitation.

Following Penn's death, the *Great Law* was overturned, and Pennsylvania resumed the use of harsh corporal punishment. But, soon afterward, Benjamin Rush, a statesman, doctor, and prison reformer, adamantly spoke out against such violent ways and tirelessly advocated that punishment should be administered as a means of reform, and not as an act of revenge.

Early U.S. Prisons

The first recognized prison in the U.S. was situated in an abandoned copper mine in Simsbury, Connecticut. The poorly conceived underground facility known as Newgate, opened in 1773, but ultimately shut down in the 1820s, due to disorganization, constant chaos, and rioting.

Around the same time, Benjamin Rush and others, including Benjamin Franklin, met with the first known reform group, the *Philadelphia Society for*

Alleviating the Miseries of Public Prisons — which later became the *Pennsylvania Prison Society* — to discuss needed reform. These efforts led to the group's first project: the Walnut Street Jail, opened in 1790, and located in Philadelphia, of which the Pennsylvania legislature reserved a wing to serve as a penitentiary for the confinement of convicted felons. Because of its humanitarian approach, a popular following ensued.

The Quakers introduced educational and religious opportunities, health services, and prison industries into the Walnut Street Jail's program. Separate living quarters were established for debtors, women, and felons, of which the most dangerous were secured in solitary cells apart from the general population. Inmates likewise worked at handicrafts, but as one might imagine, such programs fell quite short of producing sufficient income to offset the costs of incarceration.

Known as the first American penitentiary, the Walnut Street Jail permanently established the use of cellular confinement as a method to combat crime.

Unfortunately, like its predecessor, overcrowding and conflicts lead to prison unrest and violence, resulting in Walnut Street's closure in 1835. But in view of its early success years, other states used it as a model for their prisons. Penitence, work, single cells and the separation of inmates by offense type became the underpinnings of corrections in the United States.

By the late 18th century, incarceration was championed as a more humane form of punishment, at which time the first United States prisons were opened in New York, Massachusetts and Pennsylvania. Of the three, New York's Auburn Prison proved to be the most favorable model for economic productivity and other operations efficiencies. Using a Congregate workplace structure, inmates worked side-by-side, in factories, under rigid discipline and silence, by day, and in solitary confinement at night. In addition to Auburn, this model was also adopted at Ossining — better known as Sing Sing.

1915 – Warden T. M. Osborne poses in front of the flanking cell houses in Sing Sing Prison.

People from across the United States and Europe came to see the renowned Auburn Prison, and until the 1820s could purchase a prison tour for only 12 1/2 cents.

Following the Civil War, prisons were built across the country, with exception of a few southern states where road gangs and state farms remained en vogue. Prison factory production included merchandise such as shoes, barrels, carpets, engines, boilers, harnesses, clothing, and furniture sold on the open market to American consumers. Items were, likewise, exported to

Canada and Latin America as a means of financially supporting prison operations.

From the very outset of the prison industries concept, officials intended for prison labor to offset the cost of incarceration, in whole or in part.

Petty crimes, public drunkenness, and other misdemeanors would often result in sentencing to a road gang.

By the early 1900s, reformers were calling for prisons to look beyond punishment by providing offenders opportunities for rehabilitation.

And so the road was paved for the birth of numerous prison industries systems, including the Contract System, Lease System, and Piece-Price System.

Under the *Contract System*: prison officials solicited bids from private employers to hire inmate labor services, to be performed within prison confines, with prison officials retaining control over security and sustenance.

The contractor sold the finished goods in the open market, and the state received a fixed fee per prisoner, per day.

Under the *Lease System*: private employers essentially maintained control over all aspects of prison life, including security and living conditions. Work was typically performed outside the prison confines on farms, construction sites, railroads, mines, etc. Although labor leases with railroads were not lucrative, given on-the-job accidents and escapes, other types of work such as mining and farming fared well.

Under the *Piece-Price System*: the labor rate was based upon the number of finished goods completed by the inmate, and daily minimum quantities were established by prison officials.

As one might surmise, the advent of these systems bred abuses from the inside-out. While prison factories cranked out cheaply made goods, inmates worked under slave labor conditions, and profit-hungry entrepreneurs benefitted from inmate resources, thereby undercutting free labor and private business.

Eventually, private business owners allied with social reformers and loudly criticized enterprises engaged in any form of prison labor. The culmination of their allegations of abuse and escalating complaints of unfair competition led to numerous prison reform actions by the close of the 19th century.

The Advent of the Federal Prison System

Ultimately, given the ongoing controversy over the exploitation of prison labor, Congress voted to establish a separate federal prison system in 1891.

The *Three Prisons Act of 1891* was the seed from which Federal Prison Industries would germinate. The Act led to the establishment of our Nation's first federal penitentiary in 1895, at the site of an old army prison in Leavenworth, Kansas. The second institution opened in Atlanta, Georgia, in 1902, followed by a third penitentiary situated on McNeil Island in Puget Sound, Washington. Two of these three original prisons remain active within the federal system to this day — Leavenworth and Atlanta — and, in fact, USP Atlanta is one of our largest federal institutions, with a capacity of 3,000 inmates.

From 1929 through the 1940s, a series of laws limiting the shipment of prison- made goods presented new challenges in providing productive inmate employment. Of note were:

the *Hawes-Cooper Act of 1929*: which rendered prison-made goods shipped outside the state subject to the laws of the destination state;
the *Ashurst-Sumners Act of 1935*: which made it a federal offense to ship inmate- produced goods to states where their laws prohibited receipt, sale or use;
the *Walsh-Healy Act of 1936*: which banned inmate labor associated with federal procurement contracts in the manufacture, production or furnishing of any materials, supplies, articles or equipment used in government contracts exceeding $10,000;
the *Sumners-Ashurst Act of 1940*: which made it a federal crime to knowingly transport prison-made goods in interstate commerce for private use, regardless of prevailing laws in those states.

Inmates at Fort Leavenworth begin work on the foundation for the new U.S. Penitentiary in 1902.

Even as far back as the early 1900s, prison industrial programs were perceived as a threat to labor unions and business. But the newly created Federal Bureau of Prisons, established in 1930 as a component of the

Department of Justice, recognized the vital position such programs could fill in achieving its reformations goals.

Sanford Bates, first Director of the BOP, served as President (Chairman) of FPI from 1934 until 1972.

The Vision, Perseverance and Tenacity of FPI's Founders

Among the Bureau of Prisons' key objectives was a provision to ensure more progressive, humane care for federal inmates. In recognition of the role prison industry programs could serve in achieving the Bureau's reformation goals, its Director, Sanford Bates, together with Assistant Director, James V. Bennett, implemented a wide range of reforms, including a new prison industrial structure to address inmate idleness.

The Bates/Bennett team attributed the outbreak of prison disturbances in the 1930s to a lack of meaningful work programs. They embarked on a mission of corrective action, modeling their program after the "State Use" system so as to minimize interference with private industry.

They planned that products would be sold exclusively to the Federal Government, and a Board of five Directors representing outside interests, constituents, and the Attorney General, would balance and anchor the program's correctional mandates and minimize private industry impact.

James Bennett helped draft the legislation that established FPI, and became its first Assistant Director.

As carefully crafted as the program's mission and legislation were, there was no shortage of staunch outside opposition. But, thanks to President Roosevelt's personal interest in resolving this issue, and his well-honed persuasive skills, he signed the law which authorized the establishment of Federal Prison Industries, Incorporated (FPI), June 23, 1934. This was followed by Executive Order 6917, issued December 11, 1934, which formally created FPI.

Alderson Warden Mary Belle Harris, the first female warden in the BOP, poses with Eleanor Roosevelt during a tour of the institution.

January 1, 1935, FPI officially began operations as a wholly-owned corporation of the United States Government. Industrial operations at that time consisted of a textile mill which produced cotton duck cloth, a shoe factory, as well as a broom and brush operation. By its second year, FPI had branched out into other manufacturing areas including mattress production, clothing, wood/metal furniture, and rubber mats. A woolen mill, foundry and brick plant were built, as well, and laundry operations were likewise established.

A Fast-Forward Glimpse

FPI is a true success story. It is a government program that has exceeded the expectations of its creators, operates at no cost to taxpayers, and benefits millions of constituents.

Today, FPI continues to embrace and build upon the ideals of its founders three quarters of a century ago, offering more than 175 diverse products and services, encompassing over 4 million square feet of manufacturing space, and providing a fresh start for nearly 22,000 dedicated, skilled, inmate workers who are building a brighter future.

Inmates attach soles to the welting at an FPI shoe factory.

The Early Years

1934 – 1945

JUNE 23, 1934 — President Franklin D. Roosevelt signed into law the establishment of Federal Prison Industries, Incorporated (FPI). Subsequently, on December 11, 1934, his Executive Order 6917 formally created FPI as a wholly- owned corporation of the United States Government, to operate factories and employ inmates in America's federal prisons.

A five-member Board of Directors was established, comprised of representatives from business, labor, agriculture, consumer groups and the Federal Government, to uphold FPI's programmatic mission without placing undue hardship on any industry.

Franklin Delano Roosevelt

Early FPI Board members.

Employee cars fill the parking lot at USP Leavenworth in the 1930s.

FPI's work programs were modeled after the "State Use" system so as not to negatively impact the private sector. This system prohibited the sale of prison-made goods to the public, and instead, restricted sales to the Federal Government market.

In 1937, FPI realized nearly $570,000 in profits on gross sales of over $3.7 million; a particularly notable achievement obtained in a Depression year.

In the late 1930s, FPI established a fund to finance vocational training programs and job placement services. A job placement director coordinated FPI vocational training opportunities with the needs of outside industry.

An inmate stamps out machine parts during the subassembly process at the metals factory in Lewisburg.

FPI's growth was strictly controlled. The law, coupled with FPI's own regulations imposed severe competitive disadvantages, particularly during the Depression. The most notable competitive disadvantage was FPI's widespread product diversification.

By 1940, the number of inmate workers climbed to 3,400, which was 18% of the federal inmate population. FPI was well on its way to becoming a major corporation, whose growing inmate workforce was skilled in numerous trades and produced an impressive variety of goods. Revenues were also on the rise during this period.

FPI inmates at the Federal Reformatory in Chillicothe, OH attend Airplane Mechanics School in 1942.

The factory at El Reno, OK supplies cargo nets to the military during WW II.

Although incarcerated, federal inmates feel a sense of patriotism and have continually contributed to our successful war efforts.

On the eve of World War II, FPI was producing more than 70 categories of products at 25 separate shops and factories.

When the U.S. entered World War II in December, 1941, FPI was seven years old and well positioned to make a major contribution to the war effort. Working double and triple shifts, 95 percent of FPI's output was sold to the military.

FPI matured into a national asset, producing items such as bomb fins and casings, TNT cases, parachutes, cargo nets, wooden pallets, among other defense-related products which played an important role in helping win WW II.

FPI added welding, aircraft sheet metal work, shipbuilding crafts, auto/aviation mechanics, drafting and electrician training to its training programs.

Another way in which FPI contributed to the war effort was by training inmates to move directly into defense industries jobs, upon release from prison. Job placement centers were set up at several institutions which helped hundreds of inmates each year find employment.

Downturns and New Directions

1946 – 1962

A change in FPI's good fortune began, when World War II ended in 1945. The military cancelled millions of dollars in no longer needed FPI contracts. FPI was forced to cancel orders with its materials suppliers, and sales plummeted from over $17.5 million to less than $10.7 million in 1946.

After the war, FPI shifted its operations to civilian agencies including fabric production at this textile factory.

To offset the loss of military orders, FPI relied upon the healthy backlog of civilian agency orders which had built up during the War. New training programs were developed in radio communications, air conditioning, and refrigeration. Under a law passed in 1949, FPI assumed responsibility for operating factories at designated military prisons.

The Korean War, in 1950, generated renewed military business.

Inmates apply new rubber to tires as part of the reconditioning process at the FPI operation in Texarkana.

Radio operation and repair was an exciting new FPI training program in the post-war years.

In 1952, FPI sales exceeded $29 million, and the number of inmates employed reached 3,800.

Following the Korean War, FPI re-tooled factories and renovated outdated equipment to produce new products in response to changing markets. FPI opened shops at Petersburg, Terminal Island, Terre Haute, and elsewhere, that specialized in the repair, refurbishment and reconditioning of furniture, office equipment, tires, and other government property.

Earning while learning: FPI inmates perform typewriter repair during the 1960s.

An inmate is fitted with his newly manufactured prosthetic leg at the Medical Center in Springfield, MO.

FPI also introduced new vocational training programs to manufacture artificial limbs and dentures, and to perform hospital attendant work, and television repair.

1957 through 1960, FPI underwent a $5 million expansion program (financed through its sales revenues) to build and renovate its factories, vocational training buildings, warehouses, and other structures. This capital improvement program led to improved production and enhanced vocational training, characteristic of FPI during the 1960s.

The Rehabilitative Years

1963 – 1976

Rehabilitation philosophy reached its zenith in the 1960s. The Medical Model — based on the theory that inmates' criminal tendencies could be diagnosed and treated in a manner similar to physical disease — resulted in FPI's gain of greater visibility and value.

FPI inmates work on keypunch data processing at the co- correctional facility in Terminal Island.

FPI focused its efforts on developing industries which promised the greatest training potential. Included were expansion of its electronics lines such as cable assemblies at USP McNeil Island, industrial keypunch operations at FCI Terminal Island and FPC Alderson, a custom furniture factory at FPC Allenwood, and a plastics factory at USP Terre Haute. Outmoded industries, such as laundries, foundry operations and needle trades were scaled back.

The Vietnam War led to a short-term spike in FPI's production and sales levels. By the late 1 960s, military sales were offset by cutbacks in civilian agency orders, resulting in declining overall sales in 1969 and 1971. Sales further decreased at the close of the Vietnam War.

1974 marked FPI's organization into seven distinct divisions, each handling resource management, production and sales in a specific FPI industry: (1) Automated Data Processing; (2) Electronics; (3) Graphics; (4) Metals; (5) Shoe & Brush; (6) Textiles; and (7) Woods and Plastics. In tandem, regional marketing positions were established and, soon afterward, a program to improve product quality and acceptability.

By 1975, FPI increased sales through a greater emphasis on marketing and attention to customer service.

The Bureau shifted from the *Medical Model* to the *Balanced Model* of corrections. Rehabilitation was balanced against other correctional goals such as punishment, deterrence, and incapacitation. While rehabilitation ceased to be the primary objective, FPI's work and education programs continued to play a critical role under the new philosophy.

The Growth Years

1977–1989

The marketing initiatives of the mid-to-late 1970s laid the groundwork for the next three decades, as FPI intensified it focus on customer satisfaction, and aligned the organization based upon modern business principles.

1977 marked the beginning of FPI's new "identity." A new corporate logo and trade name — UNICOR — were introduced. In addition, a Corporate Marketing Office was created to develop nationwide marketing strategies and programs.

UNICOR introduced new lines in stainless steel products, thermoplastics, printed circuits, modular furniture, ergonomic chairs, Kevlar-reinforced items (such as military helmets), and optics, in an effort to increase its competitive position.

State-of-the-art production techniques were embraced, including the use of modern printing equipment to automate the production of government forms. Such efforts led to improved product offerings which, in turn, created new inmate work opportunities to better prepare inmates for post-release employment.

A Beaumont inmate drills a Kevlar helmet to specification for hardware attachment.

In 1982, the BOP directed that inmates must demonstrate a 6th grade literacy level in order to advance beyond entry level pay status. In 1986, the literacy standard was increased to the 8th grade level, and in 1991, a high school diploma, or GED certification, became the requirement.

Surges in the Bureau's inmate population occurred in the 1980s, due to increased prosecution for drug crimes, longer sentences, elimination of parole, and increased responsibility for housing aliens awaiting deportation. In turn, FPI was driven to increase the number of inmates it employed and the number of factories it operated.

An inmate locks up the metal plate on a rotary letterpress at FCI Sandstone.

Material is cut for battle dress uniforms in support of Operation Desert Storm.

Many UNICOR factories were activated and expanded during the 1980s and 1990s. Administrative operations were streamlined, product divisions were reorganized, and strategic planning principles were introduced .

UNICOR believed that all of these proactive efforts, and more, were essential to retain a strong customer position. Between 1987 and 1990, UNICOR successfully increased production by 4%, even though federal procurement decreased by 40 % during the same period (in product lines offered by UNICOR).

UNICOR excelled as a reliable, quality supplier to the Federal Government, and received accolades for its superb support in providing our troops needed items during Operations Desert Shield and Desert Storm.

The Customer Outreach Years

1990 –2004

To attract new relationships and sustain its existing customer base, UNICOR launched a spirited marketing/customer service campaign. Total customer satisfaction was reinforced throughout the organization. Marketing centers were opened across the country, product distribution depots were established, a corporate-wide quality improvement campaign was conducted, and numerous marketing outreach campaigns were implemented.

Success breeds attention and criticism, and UNICOR's accomplishments generated controversy. At the heels of the economic recession, private business elements and labor renewed a very old concern: that prison industrial programs posed a threat to both free enterprise and jobs for law-abiding citizens.

More than a half-century later, UNICOR faced the same challenges as its founders! Critics challenged UNICOR's mandatory source provision — a statutory requirement that federal agencies purchase from UNICOR if it could provide the desired products on time and at competitive prices. It was UNICOR's position that its mandatory source provision was necessary to offset several competitive disadvantages, such as its labor-intensive production environment, untrained/uneducated labor pool, security costs and production delays associated with prison operations and, of course, its restriction to a single customer.

Congress mandated that an independent market study be undertaken. One of the principal findings of the study, completed in 1991, was that UNICOR's impact on the private sector was negligible.

Another noteworthy study validated, conclusively, that UNICOR successfully achieved its mission of preparing inmates for release, and providing long term benefits to society. The Post-Release Employment Project (PREP) — a 7 year study conducted by the Bureau's Office of Research and Evaluation, compared post-release activities of a group of inmates who had participated in UNICOR programs, with those who had not.

The PREP study showed that the inmates who participated in UNICOR's industrial or educational programs were:

less likely to incur misconduct reprimands, while incarcerated;
more likely to find and keep full-time, better-paying jobs;
less likely to commit crimes following release and
24 percent less likely to return to prison than inmates who did not take advantage of UNICOR work/study programs.

By 1991, inmates were required to hold a high school diploma or GED in order to work in UNICOR.

"Thank you for calling UNICOR"— The Lexington Customer Service Center fields an average of 200 customer calls per day.

The *Customer Service Center*, established at FMC Lexington, KY, in 1994, streamlined and consolidated a number of UNICOR's central office operations. The Center centralized the corporation's order processing functions and provided a toll free, one-stop-shopping servicing hot-line, staffed by inmate tele-service agents, who fielded customers' questions regarding UNICOR orders, procedures and other general topics.

Apart from providing customer added value, the Center minimized staff resources, while expanding the inmate labor pool and offering "real world" training opportunities.

In 1996, the Bureau's Inmate Placement Program (IPP), later referred to as the Inmate Transition Program (ITP) and *Federal Inmate Bonding* initiative, were introduced to provide added peace-of-mind and encouragement for companies to hire ex- felons. The ITP provides inmates instruction in resume writing, job search, and interview skills in a "mock job fair" environment in preparation for a successful transition back to their communities. This program provides hiring incentives for corporate recruiters from some of the Nation's largest, well- known corporations.

In 2000, the corporation was re-engineered from the "inside- out." Its old operating system was replaced by sophisticated manufacturing production software to support more than 3,000 users and 100 remote factory operations located country-wide.

The Internet dramatically changed the manner and speed in which the Federal Government handled business and, in response, FPI created an award-winning website for customers and prospects to browse through its diverse products and services, place on-line orders, check order status, locate and obtain sales support representatives, request waivers, and have their questions objectively answered. FPI was truly just a "click away."

Early website development.

Inmates test their interview skills during a mock Job Fair at FCI Seagoville.

Challenges from UN ICOR's detractors continued throughout this period. In response, UNICOR's Board initiated several administrative measures, starting in 2003, to facilitate customer procurement and limit competition with the private sector and organized labor.

UNICOR's mandatory source was waived for micro-level purchases and under other identified conditions. The business practice commonly referred to as "pass- through" was eliminated (in which UNICOR would purchase finished goods from its private sector partners, if circumstances prevented UNICOR's ontime fulfillment of the customer's order).

These, and other Board initiatives, made it clear that the FPI program should move in the direction of operating with less reliance on the mandatory source. Coupled with various legislative efforts which modified the application of the mandatory source provision, UNICOR was steered further into a more competitive mode of operations.

UNICOR focused its attention on the Fleet Management and Vehicular Components, Recycling, and Services Business Groups. It explored providing services to commercial companies, domestically, that would otherwise be performed outside the United States.

Sustaining Our Future

2005 – 2009

After a three year decline, the number of inmates participating in the UNICOR program increased to 19,720 inmates in 2005; 18 percent of the work-eligible inmate population.

In response to an urgent request from the Department of Homeland Security, UNICOR's Fleet Management and Vehicular Components Business Group delivered more than 100 vehicles "convoy fashion" to the Gulf region, providing immediate assistance to law enforcement offices during the relief and recovery phases of Hurricanes Katrina and Rita.

Project Greenfed, a joint pilot project with the Arkansas Department of Environmental Quality (ADEQ) was launched, located at FCI Texarkana.

Responding to an urgent request from the Department of Homeland Security, FPI delivered more than 100 vehicles to assist with Hurricane Katrina Recovery efforts. The staff from FCI Bastrop drove the vehicles "convoy fashion" to the Gulf region, just days after the storm.

Over the past 5 years, UNICOR has recycled 185 million pounds of computers and electronic equipment

It offered Arkansas residents a cost-effective, expeditious, environmentally-sound and EPA- compliant process to recycle computer equipment. Residents were provided a toll-free number to request packaging materials, to return their unwanted equipment, which was picked up from the participant's home free of charge, and delivered to UNICOR's recycling operations.

UNICOR continued to rely less upon its mandatory source. Sales were driven by UNICOR's ability to successfully meet customer requirements. To this end, an unprecedented 99.7 percent of all waiver requests received, and 100 percent of all electronics and textiles-related waiver requests, were approved for private sector purchase.

In 2006, UNICOR activated new factories at eight locations: Hazelton, WVA; McCreary, KY; Canaan, PA; Williamsburg, SC; Victorville, CA; Coleman, FL; Herlong, CA; and Bennettsville, SC.

In preparation for the eventual end of the Iraq war, UNICOR began positioning itself for a post-war environment, by pursuing commercial services that would otherwise be performed outside the United States.

In 2007, UNICOR launched a corporate-wide branding initiative to "redefine" its program and make the connection between "what we do, and why we do it." Since then, UNICOR has continued its efforts to reinforce its pro-social value, which should encourage its constituencies to support the program, not just because it provides a quality, cost- competitive product, but because it's the "right thing to do."

UNICOR introduced its new branding initiative at the 2008 GSA Expo. Updated logos, displays and colors were unveiled by staff members in UNICOR shirts and ties. It was UNICOR's first major face lift since 1988.

During 2008, increased emphasis was placed upon release preparedness and community reentry, and as of the end of the year, 21,836 inmates worked in UNICOR programs.

UNICOR embarked on a corporate-wide campaign to become a leader in ecosensitive practices, and to set the standard for Government. To ensure that its commitment to green stays the course, a senior-level task force was formed to develop a five-year environmental plan, complete with measurable, corporate-wide objectives.

UNICOR adopted Lean Six Sigma (LSS) as its standard methodology for process improvement. In fact a new Corporate Improvement Branch was established in 2009, dedicated to positive organizational change, applying LSS methods. It is believed that this initiative will set the corporation on a solid course to become more profitable, realize improved production and delivery turnarounds, reduce inventories, and promote increased customer satisfaction.

A History Yet to Be

2009 – beyond
We believe that repatriating work currently performed outside the U.S. presents a potential growth opportunity for UNICOR. Obtaining such authority will infuse the UNICOR program with new inmate jobs without undue negative impact on the American worker.

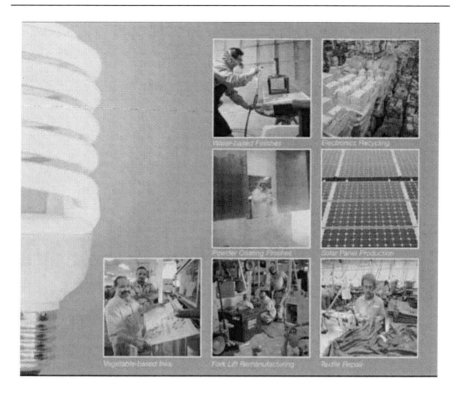

Subdued reliance on the mandatory source, increased emphasis in services and other non-mandatory source areas, combined with ongoing research to discover new markets, will lead to additional meaningful work opportunities that will keep inmates constructively occupied during incarceration, and increase their prospects for success, upon release from prison.

Green thinking and practices will remain fully ingrained in our culture, and evident in all we do.

From our suppliers and the raw materials we purchase, to our production facilities, manufacturing processes, packaging, distribution and our end products, themselves — respect for the environment will remain an integral way in which we continue to do business, from the "inside-out."

Today's "survival of the fittest" business environment necessitates that we discover the key to earn our customers' continued support, despite the competition's lure. To this end, our marketing outreach efforts will be reinforced to ensure that we keep in step with customers' changing priorities.

We will continue to educate Federal Government agencies, customers, the private sector, and other constituents about the incredible investment UNICOR represents in all of our futures. Since 1934, UNICOR is one government program that has continued to work in every sense of the word, leading to residual, lasting benefits...

a reduction in government spending;
positive impact upon the U.S. economy;
the viability and health of our communities;
the safety and security of our Nation's corrections facilities; and a
fresh start for a brighter future.

What better way to put federal procurement dollars to work! UNICOR is life changing.

SPREAD THE WORD

What Everyone Should Know about Us

We're a program, not a business. Although we produce products and perform services, the program's real output is inmates who are more likely to return to society as law-abiding taxpayers because of the job skills training and work experience received in UNICOR.

UNICOR has a positive impact on recidivism. Inmates who work in UNICOR are less likely to return to a life of crime after they are released. Research shows that inmates in UNICOR are 24% less likely to recidivate than their counterparts who did not participate in the program. Working in UNICOR has an even greater positive impact on minority offenders who are at the greatest statistical risk of recidivism.

UNICOR has a positive impact on employment success. Research shows that inmates in the program are 14% more likely to find and maintain a job than those without UNICOR experience.

UNICOR provides a program of constructive industrial work, providing sound job skills and positive work habits to inmates.

Inmates gain work skills and experience in UNICOR. Many of them have never before held a job. FPI teaches a basic work ethic. In addition to working on the factory floor, inmates also acquire computer and business skills working in the business office.

UNICOR operates at no cost to taxpayers, is entirely self sustaining, and receives no appropriated funds from Congress.

Each year, UNICOR inmates contribute almost $3 million of their earnings toward meeting financial obligations (court-ordered fines, child support, and/or victim restitution). Many also contribute toward family support and welfare by sending home a portion of their earnings.

UNICOR supports private vendors, especially small business. In 2008, 80% of its revenues was directed to the private sector in purchases of raw materials, supplies, equipment and services. And, traditionally, small business procurement (businesses owned by women, minorities, and those who are disadvantaged) have accounted for more than 60% of UNICOR purchases — nearly three times the SBA goal for federal agencies.

UNICOR is a critical correctional program within the Bureau of Prisons, serving as an essential correctional management tool. It provides constructive job skills training and work experience, which eliminates inmate idleness and greatly assists in the safe and efficient operation of the institution. Inmates in UNICOR are less likely to be involved in misconduct while incarcerated.

UNICOR "walks the talk" in green manufacturing. It is committed to a corporate-wide effort to be a leader in eco-sensitive manufacturing, from the finishes, fabrics and materials used, to the refurbishment, re-manufacture, and recycling operations that are in place among its core products and services.

ORGANIZATIONALLY SPEAKING

UNICOR's Diverse Components

The UNICOR Business Groups

The Clothing and Textiles Group (CTG) provides a wide range of products, the majority of which are procured from a distinct cadre of customers on a contractual basis. Individual orders can likewise be placed through the CTG's on-line store. Items include military clothing such as army combat uniforms, physical fitness apparel, shirts and cold weather gear. In addition, specialty bags (for helmets, tools and the United States Postal Service), body armor, gloves, household items (mattresses, towels, linens, custom drapes, bedspreads), as well as screen printing, embroidery services and textile repair services are offered.

The Electronics Business Group (EBG) is heavily relied upon by the Nation's military to provide cost-effective, precision manufacturing. Product lines include cable assemblies and wire harnesses, circuit boards, electrical components and connectors, lighting and power distribution, fiber optics, communications and plastics/molding technologies and, more recently, solar panel manufacturing.

The Fleet Solutions Group (FSG) provides a complete range of fleet modernization and remanufacturing programs including tactical vehicle and vehicular components manufacturing (RESET/RECAP), retrofitting and conversion services, as well as fleet asset services.

The Industrial Products Group (IPG) offers a diverse range of products which include agency seals, traffic /architectural signs, vehicle tags, name plates/tags, filtration services, and lockers, pallet racking and catwalks, prescription and safety eyewear, security fencing, as well as a wide variety of recognition and promotional products.

The Office Furniture Group (OFG) offers a full spectrum of products to furnish virtually any environment, from reception/lounge areas, dormitory settings and medical offices, to executive suites. Product lines include systems/modular workstations, wood case goods, file and storage offerings, office accessories, and seating appropriate for all venues. And all OFG factories have achieved ISO 9001 :2000 certification.

The Recycling Business Group (RBG) offers electronics recycling which meets all federal, state and local requirements. If an item cannot be reused, it is broken down into recyclable component parts. The RBG is ISO 9001:2000 certified by the International Standards Organization. Currently, eight processing centers and six collection sites are located throughout the country, and during Fiscal Year 2008, the RBG processed more than 37 million pounds of obsolete and excess electronics from both the private and public sectors which saved precious landfill space.

The Services Business Group (SBG) offers a full range of services which include data and document conversion, digitizing, electronic imaging, printing and bindery, contact center/help desk support, forward/reverse logistics, as well as warehousing and distribution.

UNICOR Administration and Operations

Corporate Management ensures the successful oversight and administration of the UNICOR program. It coordinates a wide variety of field and central office operations including the strategic management process, various personnel-related functions, policy oversight, legislative compliance, as well as congressional communications and reporting.

The Continuous Improvement Branch (CIB) created in 2008, is the most recent addition to UNICOR. CIB is responsible for championing positive change by applying Lean Six Sigma methods which will drive the corporation towards becoming more profitable, efficient and customer-focused.

The Financial Management Branch (FMB) ensures financial data integrity for the corporation, as a whole. It provides relevant, timely and accurate financial reporting and guidance to Corporate Management and UNICOR's Board of Directors to assist them in making informed financial decisions and cost-effective planning for the organization.

The Interagency Solutions and Procurement Branch (ISPB) provides contractual oversight for UNICOR's central office components and assists the business groups with various contractual matters, as required. In addition, this branch provides and facilitates contractual services for other government agencies in support of UNICOR's mission.

The Management Information Systems Branch (MISB) provides computer infrastructure support for UNICOR's field facilities and central office. MISB facilitates access to enterprise resource planning systems, financial management systems, and all aspects of our manufacturing processes through Systems Applications Products in Data Processing (SAP).

The Strategic Business Development & Marketing Branch (SBDM) is responsible for planning, research, market/economic analyses, external communications, corporate-level marketing, constituent relations, and customer service for the corporation.

Market analysis activities include preparation of Market Share and Sales Reports, oversight of the industry "guidelines" process for new products, economic impact studies and responding to external requests for information.

SBDM's *corporate marketing and communications* functions include traditional market development efforts to promote UNICOR's image and tell its "story" to a diverse customer and constituent base. They include trade shows and special events, publications including the corporation's Annual Report, advertising and promotional efforts, customer training and outreach. Oversight and maintenance of UNICOR's web site and on-line stores are also handled within the SBDM.

SBDM also oversees *The Customer Service Center*, launched in 1994. Located at FMC Lexington, KY, it serves as the primary liaison between UNICOR factories nationwide, and thousands of current and potential customers. Inmate tele-service agents field general customer inquiries through the Center's toll-free hotline. Order processing functions, including assignment to the appropriate manufacturing locations for production, are also performed.

Visit our website at *unicor.gov* for more information.

OVERSIGHT THROUGH THE YEARS

BOP Directors 1930 – 2009	Assistant Directors for Industries 1930 – 2009	FPI Board Members 1934 – 2009		
Sanford Bates 1930-1937	James V.Bennett 1934-1937	**Original Members Appointed by President Roosevelt:**	Dr. William E. Morgan 1966-1996	Donald R. Elliott 2002-present
James V. Bennett 1937-1964	A.H. Conner 1938-1960	Sanford Bates 1934-1972	Arthur H. White 1997-2002	**Representing Retailers & Consumers**
Myrl E.Alexander 1964-1970	Fred T. Wilkinson 1960-1961	Dr. Marion L. Brittain 1934-1952	David D. Spears 2002-present	Sam A. Lewisohn 1934-1951
Norman A. Carlson 1970-1987	Preston G. Smith 1961-1965	Sam A. Lewisohn 1934-1951	**Representing the Secretary of Defense**	James L. Palmer 1951-1976
J. Michael Quinlan 1987-1992	T. Wade Markley 1965-1966		E. Earle Rives 1949-1953	Monica Herrera Smith 1979-1984

Kathleen M.
Hawk-Sawyer
1992-2003

Harley G.
Lappin
2003-Present

Olin C.
Minton
1967-1969

J.T.
Willingham
1969-1971
John J. Clark
1971-1972

Loy S. Hayes
1972-1973

David C.
Jelinek
1974-1979

Gerald Farkas
1979-1989

Richard Seiter
1989-1993

Steve Schwalb
1993-2007

Paul M. Laird
2007-Present

Thomas A.
Rickert
1934-1941

Judge John B.
Miller
1934-1937

**Representing
the Attorney
General**

Sanford Bates
1934-1972

Peter B.
Bensinger
1974-1984

Richard Abell
1985-1990

Shirley D.
Peterson
1991-1992

Harry H.
Flickinger
1992-1992

Stephen R.
Colgate
1994-2001

Dr. Paul R.
Corts
2003-2006

Lee J. Lofthus
2007-present

**Representing
Agriculture**

Judge John B.
Miller
1934-1937

Emil Schram
1938-1966

Frank A. Reid
1953-1959
John Marshall
Briley
1960-1988

Robert Q.
Millan
1989-1996

Todd A.
Weiler
1996-1999

Deidre A. Lee
2000-2001

Diane K.
Morales
2002-2004

P. Jackson
Bell
2007-2009

**Representing
Industry**

Dr. Marion L.
Brittain
1934-1951

Berry N.
Beaman
1954-1976

Daryl F.
Grisham
1979-1982

Paul T. Shirley
1982-1990

Mark J.
D'Aarcangelo
1991-1995

Susan A.
Loewenberg
1995-2002

Donald A.
Schwartz
1985-1992
Thomas N.
Tripp
1993-1994

Joseph M.
Aragon
1994-2002

Audrey J.
Roberts
2002-present

**Representing
Labor**

Thomas A.
Rickert
1934-1941

Robet J. Watt
1943-1947

George Meany
1947-1979

Lane Kirkland
1980-1988

Kenneth
Young
1994-1995

Richard G.
Womack
1996-2002

Kenneth R.
Rocks
2002-2005

Franklin G.
Gale
2007-present

AS A MATTER OF FACT...

Some Little-Known Facts Of Interest From Unicor's Past and Present

- **December 27, 1934**
  The first FPI Board of Directors meeting was held.
- **A Boy Scout Tour**
  When touring a Minnesota prison with his Boy Scout troop, long time champion of UNICOR, Chief Justice Warren Burger first became interested in prison industries as a child.
- **4 Million Square Feet**
  UNICOR's expanse of manufacturing and services facilities.
- **700**
  The number of mock job fairs held, to date, in more than 100 prisons.
- **$900,000**
  Inmate scholarship funds awarded since 2000.
- **32.5 Million Tons**
  Scrap kept from America's landfills thanks to UNICOR's "green" practices.
- **8**
  The number of UNICOR logos used to identify UNICOR, to date.

ACKNOWLEDGMENTS

Thank you!

Our 75th Anniversary edition, "Factories with Fences: 75Years of Changing Lives," was made possible thanks tothe research, planning, creative writing and designefforts of many.

Sincere appreciation goes to Bureau of PrisonsArchivist, Anne Diestel, for her invaluable assistance inproviding the many wonderful, historic photos shownthroughout this edition.

Special kudos go the UNICOR Strategic BusinessDevelopment and Marketing team of Jan Hynson, MarkMiller and Jim Wishart, who breathed new dimensionand life into the wonderful original 1996 edition of"Factories With Fences," rendering it up to date at the perfect time to commemorate UNICOR's 75thAnniversary.

Finally, we thank and acknowledge UNICOR's PrintPlant at FCC Petersburg, VA, for its expertise in printingthis publication.

CHAPTER SOURCES

Chapter 1 - This is an edited, reformatted and augmented version of a U.S. Department of Justice, Federal Bureau of Prisions publication, dated January 2011.

Chapter 2 - This is an edited, reformatted and augmented version of a Congressional Research Service publication, R41525, dated December 9, 2010.

Chapter 3 - This is an edited, reformatted and augmented version of a Congressional Research Service publication, RL32380, dated January 4, 2011.

Chapter 1 - This is an edited, reformatted and augmented version of a Unicor, Federal Prision Industries, Inc. publication.

INDEX

A

abuse, 20, 21, 22, 26, 27, 34, 44, 71
access, 5, 6, 30, 33, 54, 57, 97
accommodations, 6
accountability, 3, 4, 56
adjustment, 9, 13
administrators, 14
adult literacy, 19
age, 29
agencies, viii, 13, 47, 48, 52, 53, 55, 56,
    58, 59, 63, 64, 80, 86, 93, 95, 97
agriculture, 49, 65, 76
alcohol use, 32
alienation, 65
anger, 6
appropriations, 20, 29, 47, 50
Appropriations Act, 55
arrest, 42
assault, 44
assets, 7, 8
attachment, 84
authority, 60, 92
automate, 84

B

barriers, 17
base, 30, 35, 86, 98
basic education, 31

benefits, 62, 75, 87, 94
bias, 23
board members, 49, 58
boilers, 69
business environment, 93
businesses, 48, 53, 56, 57, 95

C

campaigns, 86
certification, 85, 96
Chad, 42
challenges, 2, 5, 61, 72, 86
chaos, 67
Chief Justice, 61, 62, 100
CIA, 48
citizens, 7, 8
Civil War, 61, 69
classes, 11
classification, 3
cleaning, 12
climate, 57
Clinton Administration, 59
closure, 68
clothing, 50, 69, 75, 95
cognitive skills, 6
commerce, 59, 72
commercial, 65, 89, 91
communication, 4
communities, 7, 12, 29, 88, 94

community, vii, 1, 5, 6, 9, 10, 11, 12, 13,
    15, 16, 17, 20, 21, 22, 31, 32, 44,
    92
community service, 20
compensation, 60
competition, 55, 57, 58, 71, 89, 93
competitive advantage, 48
compliance, 60, 97
computer, 91, 94, 97
conditioning, 80
confinement, vii, 1, 9, 12, 21, 68, 69
congressional budget, 29
Consolidated Appropriations Act, 55
constituents, 73, 75, 93
construction, 3, 63, 71
consumers, 49, 69
control group, 23, 24
conviction, 38, 41, 44
copper, 67
cost, vii, 1, 4, 12, 15, 16, 20, 52, 70, 75,
    91, 94, 96, 97
cotton, 74
counseling, 6, 7, 8, 12, 13, 17
crimes, 20, 31, 70, 85, 87
criminal activity, 1
criminal justice system, 2
criminal tendencies, 82
criminals, 31
criticism, 61, 86
culture, 93
customer service, 83, 86, 97
customers, 88, 93, 95, 98

D

daily living, 6
data analysis, 9
data processing, 83
debtors, 68
debts, 50, 66
deficit, 6
dentures, 82
Department of Defense, 48, 55
Department of Homeland Security, 90

Department of Justice (DOJ), v, 1, 5, 17,
    28, 42, 43, 44, 48, 51, 59, 60, 73
dependent variable, 34
detainees, 18, 44
detection, 17
detention, 1, 3
deterrence, 83
directives, 57
directors, 54
disorder, 21
displacement, 60
distribution, 86, 93, 96
District of Columbia, 44, 59
diversification, 78
downsizing, 53
draft, 74
drug abuse, vii, viii, 10, 15, 16, 20, 21,
    22, 25, 26, 27, 30, 31, 34, 42
drug education, 20, 26
drug offense, 44
drug treatment, 9, 10, 12
drugs, 3, 21, 24, 25, 26, 27, 34, 35, 37,
    38, 40, 41, 42

E

earnings, 7, 8, 18, 95
education, vii, viii, 6, 9, 10, 11, 13, 15,
    16, 18, 19, 20, 21, 22, 25, 26, 27,
    30, 34, 43, 61, 83
educational programs, 18, 87
emergency, 4, 13
emergency preparedness, 4
employees, 2, 3, 5, 57
employers, 58, 70, 71
employment, viii, 5, 10, 11, 17, 20, 47,
    48, 56, 62, 72, 79, 84, 94
encoding, 50
encouragement, 88
enforcement, 13
entrepreneurs, 71
environment, 4, 8, 12, 17, 52, 86, 88, 91,
    93, 96
EPA, 91
equipment, 47, 50, 60, 72, 81, 84, 91, 95

erosion, 53
ethics, 5
Europe, 69
evidence, 20, 21, 29
exclusion, 18
execution, 66
Executive Order, 53, 58, 66, 74, 76
expertise, 100
exploitation, 71

F

factories, 6, 18, 30, 49, 57, 62, 63, 69,
    71, 76, 79, 80, 81, 82, 85, 86, 91,
    96, 98
faith, 6
families, 13, 65
family support, 60, 95
farming techniques, 64
farms, 69, 71
federal agency, 20
Federal Government, 5, 31, 47, 48, 49,
    53, 57, 59, 63, 65, 73, 76, 77, 86,
    88, 93
fencing, 96
fiber, 96
fiber optics, 96
filtration, 96
financial, 7, 8, 17, 50, 60, 63, 95, 97
financial data, 97
financial support, 63
flexibility, 21
fluctuations, 2
food, 6, 30, 63
force, 92
formula, 35
funding, 30, 47, 50
funds, 48, 55, 94, 100

G

gangs, 69
general knowledge, 19
Georgia, 71

goods and services, 63
government spending, 94
Great Depression, 61
group activities, 44
growth, 2, 3, 78, 92
GSA, 92
guidance, 7, 97
guidelines, 31, 97

H

health, 5, 13, 59, 68, 94
health care, 5
health education, 13
health services, 68
high school, 18, 19, 24, 25, 26, 27, 28,
    31, 34, 37, 38, 40, 41, 85, 87
high school diploma, 18, 19, 24, 25, 26,
    27, 28, 31, 34, 37, 38, 40, 41, 85,
    87
hiring, 88
history, 21, 31, 32, 44, 49, 59
homicide, 44
House, 58, 59
housing, 3, 17, 85
Hurricane Katrina, 90

I

ideals, 75
identification, 5
identity, 84
image, 98
immigration, 3
imprisonment, 1, 6, 10, 13, 43, 67
improvements, 65
incarceration, 5, 7, 8, 22, 26, 44, 57, 68,
    70, 93
income, 12, 50, 68
independent variable, 35
individuals, 57, 58, 59
industries, viii, 6, 9, 19, 22, 47, 48, 49,
    51, 52, 58, 61, 62, 68, 70, 79, 83,
    100

industry, 18, 23, 49, 54, 58, 60, 61, 62, 64, 65, 73, 76, 77, 83, 97
infrastructure, 97
institutions, vii, 1, 2, 3, 4, 6, 10, 11, 13, 20, 21, 22, 30, 43, 57, 60, 71, 79
instructional time, 19
integrity, 97
interference, 73
internal controls, 3
intervention, 23
investment, 93
issues, 3, 5, 13, 16, 17, 29, 48, 56

J

job skills, 6, 49, 63, 94, 95
job training, 18
judiciary, 31
jurisdiction, 17
justification, 44
juveniles, 12

L

landfills, 100
Latin America, 70
law enforcement, 2, 13, 90
laws, 5, 31, 49, 53, 61, 72
lead, 5, 52, 62, 68, 93
learning, 50, 81
legislation, 2, 48, 53, 65, 66, 74
legislative authority, 60
light, 14, 31
ii, 15, 16, 19, 25, 26, 27, 28, 34, 43, 85
living conditions, 71
local community, 13
logistics, 96

M

machinery, 59
majority, 8, 95
management, 4, 5, 6, 17, 18, 44, 50, 95, 97

manufacturing, 53, 56, 57, 75, 88, 93, 95, 96, 97, 98, 100
market share, 55
marketability, 59
marketing, 83, 84, 86, 93, 97, 98
marketing initiatives, 84
marketplace, 53
marriage, 13
mass, 13, 56
mass media, 13
materials, 60, 72, 79, 91, 95
matter, iv, 52, 65
measurement, 42
medical, 3, 6, 12, 30, 96
medical care, 30
medical reason, 6
mental impairment, 22
merchandise, 69
metals, 77
methodology, 24, 92
military, 44, 63, 79, 80, 83, 84, 95, 96
minorities, 95
minority groups, 9
mission, vii, 15, 16, 29, 42, 63, 73, 74, 76, 87, 97
missions, 3
models, 4, 5, 34, 35, 42
modernization, 96
monopoly, 52
mutilation, 66

N

National Defense Authorization Act, 48, 54, 55
National Park Service, 12

O

offenders, vii, viii, 1, 3, 9, 10, 12, 15, 16, 30, 33, 47, 48, 59, 62, 70, 94
officials, 70, 71
open markets, 59
operating system, 88

operations, 3, 6, 14, 29, 31, 49, 56, 58, 63, 65, 66, 69, 70, 74, 80, 83, 86, 88, 89, 91, 95, 97
opportunities, vii, 5, 6, 11, 15, 16, 26, 49, 52, 56, 57, 68, 70, 77, 84, 88, 93
opt out, 19, 43
organized labor, 60, 89
outreach, 62, 86, 93, 98
oversight, vii, 1, 30, 48, 56, 97

P

parenting, 6
parole, 3, 20, 30, 31, 42, 44, 59, 85
parole board, 31
participants, 9
patriotism, 79
peace, 88
peer review, 42
permit, 13, 18
Philadelphia, 67
physical features, 3
physical fitness, 95
plastics, 83, 96
playing, 52
policy, 18, 20, 30, 43, 44, 49, 97
population, 2, 3, 5, 6, 17, 21, 28, 29, 30, 33, 44, 51, 53, 58, 63, 68, 78, 85, 90
population growth, 3
potential benefits, 57
preparation, iv, 6, 63, 88, 91, 97
preparedness, 92
President, 49, 65, 66, 73, 74, 76, 98
principles, 58, 84, 86
prison environment, 58
prisoners, 17, 20, 43, 49, 58
prisons, vii, 1, 2, 10, 13, 14, 15, 16, 17, 30, 32, 33, 44, 48, 49, 50, 59, 68, 69, 70, 71, 76, 80, 100
probability, 15, 16, 26, 27, 29, 33, 35
profit, 59, 71

programming, vii, 6, 10, 15, 16, 17, 21, 22, 23, 24, 25, 26, 29, 30, 32, 35, 42
project, 20, 68, 90
public awareness, 13
public safety, 1, 2, 9, 14
public sector, 96
public service, 14
public welfare, 31
public-private partnerships, 57
punishment, 45, 66, 67, 68, 70, 83

Q

Quakers, 68
quality improvement, 86

R

radio, 80
random assignment, 23
rape, 44
raw materials, 93, 95
reading, 19
reality, 13, 62
reception, 96
recession, 58, 86
recidivism, 6, 9, 10, 11, 13, 23, 47, 49, 51, 52, 62, 94
recidivism rate, 10, 13, 47, 51
recognition, 62, 73, 96
recommendations, iv
reconditioning, 80, 81
recovery, 90
recreational, 63
recycling, 50, 91, 95, 96
reform, 61, 62, 67, 71
Reform, 3, 52
reformers, 70, 71
reforms, 73
regression, 26, 34, 35, 42
regression model, 34, 35, 42
regulations, 5, 55, 58, 78
rehabilitation, 23, 31, 49, 65, 67, 70, 83

Rehabilitation Act, 43
rehabilitation program, 23
relief, 90
repair, 59, 63, 81, 82, 95
requirements, 6, 12, 30, 53, 55, 58, 59,
    60, 91, 96
researchers, 23, 24, 52
resolution, 52
resource management, 83
resources, vii, 16, 29, 71, 88
response, 33, 81, 88, 89, 90
restitution, 7, 8, 65, 95
restrictions, 32, 59
restructuring, 10
revenue, 47, 50
risk, 3, 9, 13, 50, 94
risk factors, 3
roots, 61
rubber, 75, 80
rules, 5, 31, 45

S

safety, 2, 3, 4, 5, 6, 10, 29, 63, 65, 94, 96
sample design, 33
sampling error, 52
SAP, 97
scholarship, 100
school, 12, 19, 25, 28
scope, 57
Secretary of Defense, 54, 55, 58, 98
security, 2, 3, 4, 5, 6, 10, 12, 13, 17, 30,
    33, 50, 59, 63, 70, 71, 86, 94, 96
seed, 71
self-improvement, vii, 6, 7, 8, 15, 16
seminars, 62
Senate, 53, 59
sentencing, 2, 21, 30, 44, 66, 70
Sentencing Guidelines, 45
sexual abuse, 44
shortage, 74
signs, 96
skills training, 10, 22, 61, 63
small businesses, 48, 52, 53, 57
society, vii, 15, 16, 87, 94

software, 88
staff members, 92
staffing, 3, 30
standard error, 33, 34
state, 13, 32, 44, 57, 58, 59, 60, 69, 70,
    72, 96
statutes, 53
statutory authority, 53, 58
steel, 84
stigma, 61
storage, 96
strategic management, 97
strategic planning, 86
stratified sampling, 33
structural barriers, 4
structure, vii, 16, 17, 30, 31, 69, 73
subsistence, 12
substance abuse, 6, 13, 18, 20, 32, 44
supervision, 3, 4, 9
supervisors, 5, 50
supplier, 86
suppliers, 65, 79, 93
surveillance, 4
survival, 93
sweat, 6

T

taxes, 60
taxpayers, 75, 94
teachers, 5
techniques, 11, 84
technologies, 4, 56, 96
technology, 48, 56
telephone, 13
tension, 57
tenure, 62
textiles, 50, 91
thermoplastics, 84
torture, 66
trade, viii, 43, 47, 48, 50, 54, 56, 84, 98
training, viii, 9, 11, 13, 18, 19, 20, 23,
    47, 48, 49, 61, 63, 77, 79, 80, 81,
    82, 83, 88, 94, 95, 98
training programs, 79, 80

transcripts, 11
transport, 59, 67, 72
treatment, vii, viii, 6, 9, 10, 12, 15, 16,
    18, 20, 21, 22, 23, 24, 25, 26, 27,
    30, 31, 32, 34, 44
trial, 35, 66

U

U.S. economy, 56, 94
U.S. Treasury, 59
UN, 89
unions, 63, 72
United, 43, 59, 62, 68, 69, 74, 76, 89, 91,
    95
United States, 43, 59, 62, 68, 69, 74, 76,
    89, 91, 95
universities, 12

V

variables, 23, 25, 33, 34, 42
vehicles, 90
Vice President, 59
victims, 8
Vietnam, 83
violence, 68
violent crime, 31
vision, 62

vocational education, 22
vocational training, 6, 9, 13, 18, 23, 77,
    82
Volunteers, 13

W

wages, 9, 47, 50, 57, 60, 63, 65
waiver, 58, 59, 91
war, 62, 79, 80, 81, 91
war years, 81
Washington, 42, 43, 44, 59, 60, 71
weapons, 3
wear, 6
web, 98
welding, 79
welfare, 95
wood, 75, 96
work ethic, 6, 18, 62, 94
worker benefits, 60
workers, 3, 4, 57, 58, 60, 75, 78
workforce, 58, 78
workplace, 56, 69
World War I, 61, 79

Y

young adults, 12

786018